EASY READING SELECTIONS IN ENGLISH

ROBERT J. DIXSON

EASY READING SELECTIONS IN

ENGLISH

A NEW REVISED EDITION

Regents Publishing Company, Inc.

Cover design: Paul Gamarello
Text design: Suzanne Bennett & Associates
Illustrations: Constance Maltese

Copyright © 1984 by R. J. Dixson Associates

ISBN 0-88345-538-2

Published by Regents Publishing Company, Inc.
2 Park Avenue
New York, New York 10016

Printed in the United States of America

10 9 8 7 6 5

Preface

This revised edition of *Easy Reading Selections in English* provides short stories from around the world for high-intermediate to advanced students of English as a second language. In most instances, the stories have been simplified.

Students not sufficiently advanced should prepare by using the following texts: *Beginning Lessons in English* (Parts A and B), *Exercises in English Conversation,* and *Graded Exercises in English* (a general grammar supplement). The selections in this book should not be attempted by beginning students; otherwise, studying the text will become a tedious exercise in translation.

Most of the selections are well-known stories by classic authors. Long-time users of *Easy Reading Selections* will detect a change in format from previous editions. Each unit is roughly the same length (8–12 pages), and each is followed by the same kinds of exercises.

Comprehension questions follow Parts One and Two. These twenty questions, and any others a teacher may supplement them with, immediately test whether the students have a basic understanding of the story. Teachers should pay close attention to vocabulary, since not all students will understand all the terms used in the stories. The exercises should be written and, in general, should be supplemented whenever possible by questions of a similar nature or theme. Generally, the exercises use terms and structures from the story, so teachers have an additional opportunity to check understanding of vocabulary and grammar. Repetition with direct, complete, and automatic answers is important. If answers to a particular exercise are slow or hesitant, teachers should repeat the questions.

The discussion questions are new in this edition. Teachers may use them for written work or for conversational purposes to stimulate the students to use the vocabulary and structures from the stories, as well as to generate new thoughts.

Easy Reading Selections is the second in a series of three readers. The first, *Elementary Reader in English*, is a reader for beginning and low-intermediate students. The third reader, *Modern Short Stories*, is for advanced students. The same plan of presentation is followed in all three books: selected readings, graded as to level of difficulty, with vocabulary, structure, and conversational exercises.

Contents

Unit 1: The Last Leaf

O. Henry

O. Henry is the pen name for a short story writer named William Sidney Porter (1862–1910). His stories often resemble newspaper articles, and they usually end with an interesting twist.

PART ONE

Many people who are interested in art come to Greenwich Village, which is a section of New York City. They like the Bohemian life of the village, and they enjoy living among so many artists. The buildings and apartments are often very old and dirty, but this only adds to the interest of the place.

At the top of an old, three-story brick house, Sue and Johnsy had their studio. One of them was from the state of Maine, the other from California. They had met in the restaurant of an Eighth Street hotel. Both were artists who had recently come to New York to make their living.

1

That was in May. In November, a cold, unseen stranger, whom the doctors called pneumonia, visited the city, touching one here and one there with his icy finger.

He touched Johnsy and she lay, scarcely moving, on her painted iron bed, looking through the small window at the blank wall of the opposite building.

One morning the busy doctor invited Sue into the hall.

"She has about one chance in ten to live," he said as he shook down the mercury in his clinical thermometer. "And that one chance depends upon her desire to get better. But your little friend has made up her mind that she is going to die. Is she worrying about something?"

"She wanted to paint a picture of the Bay of Naples some day," said Sue.

"No, something more important—a man perhaps?"

"No."

"Well, perhaps it is a result of her fever and her general physical weakness. But when a patient begins to feel sure that she is going to die, then I subtract fifty percent from the power of medicines. If you can succeed in making her interested in something, in asking, for instance, about the latest exhibit at a local gallery or some other art news, then I can promise you a one-in-five chance for her instead of one-in-ten."

After the doctor had gone, Sue went into her own room and cried. Later, trying not to show her sadness, she went into Johnsy's room, whistling.

Johnsy lay under the bedclothes, with her face toward the window. Sue stopped whistling, thinking Johnsy was asleep. But soon Sue heard a low sound, several times repeated. Sue went quickly to the bedside.

Johnsy's eyes were wide open. She was looking out of the window and counting backwards.

"Twelve," she said, and a little later, "eleven," and then "ten" and "nine," and then "eight—seven."

Sue looked out of the window. What was Johnsy counting? There was only a gray backyard and the blank wall of the opposite house. An old, old vine, dead at the roots, climbed halfway up the wall. The cold breath of autumn had blown almost all the leaves from the vine until its branches were almost bare.

"What is it, dear?" asked Sue.

"Six," said Johnsy very quietly. "They are falling faster now. Three days ago there were almost a hundred. It makes my head ache to count them. But now it's easy. There goes another one. There are only five left now."

"Five what, dear? Tell me!" said Sue.

"Leaves. The leaves of that vine. When the last leaf of that vine falls, I must go, too. I've known that for three days. Didn't the doctor tell you?"

"The doctor didn't say any such thing. That is pure foolishness," said Sue. "What connection have those old leaves with your getting well? And you used to love that old vine so much. Please don't be silly. The doctor told me this morning that your chances of getting well soon were excellent. Now try to take some of your soup and let me get back to work so that I can make money to buy you some good port wine."

"There's no use buying any more wine," said Johnsy, keeping her eyes fixed on the blank wall of the house opposite. "There goes another leaf. That leaves just four. I want to see the last one fall before it gets dark. Then I'll go, too."

"Johnsy, dear," said Sue, bending over her, "will you promise me to keep your eyes closed and not look out of the window until I have finished working? I must deliver these drawings tomorrow. I need the light; otherwise I would pull down the curtain."

"Can't you draw in your room?" said Johnsy coldly.

"I'd rather stay here with you," said Sue. "Besides, I don't want you to keep looking at those silly leaves."

"Tell me as soon as you have finished," said Johnsy, closing her eyes and lying white and still. "Because I want to see the last leaf fall. I'm tired of waiting. I'm tired of thinking."

"Try to sleep," said Sue a little later. "I must go downstairs for a minute to get Mr. Behrman, who is going to sit as my model. But I will be right back. And don't move, and also please promise me not to look out of the window."

Comprehension

1. What is a *pen name?* What was O. Henry's real name?
2. Where does this story take place? Why is it an interesting place?
3. What are the names of the two young women in the story?
4. How do the women make a living?
5. What was Johnsy's illness?
6. Why did the doctor believe that Johnsy's desire to live was important?

7. What did the doctor think Johnsy's chances were?
8. How did he think her chances could be improved?
9. Why was Johnsy counting the falling leaves? What did she think would happen when the last leaf fell?
10. Why did Sue have to leave the room?

PART TWO

Old Mr. Behrman was a painter who lived on the first floor beneath Johnsy and Sue. He was more than sixty years old. Behrman was a failure in art. He had always wanted to paint a masterpiece, but he had never begun to paint it. For many years he had painted nothing, except now and then a piece of commercial or advertising work. He earned a little money by serving as a model for those young artists who could not pay the price for a regular model. He drank a great deal of whiskey and, when he was drunk, always talked about the great masterpiece he was going to paint. He was a fierce, intense little man who considered himself as a watchdog and protector for the two young artists living above him, of whom he was very fond.

Sue found Behrman in his poorly lighted studio. In one corner of the room stood a blank canvas which had been waiting for twenty-five years to receive the first line of the promised masterpiece. Sue told him of the strange idea which Johnsy had concerning the last leaf, and said that she feared that Johnsy would really die when the last leaf fell.

Old Behrman shouted, "Are there people in the world who are foolish enough to die simply because leaves fall from an old vine? I have never heard of such a thing. Why do you permit such silly ideas to come into her mind? Oh, that poor little Miss Johnsy."

"She is very ill and very weak," explained Sue, "and the fever has left her mind full of strange ideas."

Johnsy was sleeping when they both went upstairs. Sue pulled down the curtain and motioned to Behrman to go into the other room. There they looked out of the window fearfully at the vine. Then they looked at each other for a moment without speaking. A cold rain was falling, mixed with snow. Behrman took a seat and prepared himself to pose for Sue as a model.

When Sue woke up the next morning, she found Johnsy with dull, wide open eyes, looking at the window.

"Put up the curtain. I want to see," Johnsy said quietly.

Sue obeyed.

4

But, oh, after the heavy rain and the strong wind, one leaf was still hanging on the vine. The last leaf. Still dark green, it hung from a branch some twenty feet above the ground.

"It is the last one," said Johnsy. "I thought it would surely fall during the night. I heard the wind and the rain. It will fall today and I shall die at the same time."

"Dear Johnsy," said Sue, placing her face close to Johnsy's on the pillow, "think of me if you won't think of yourself. What shall I do?"

The day passed slowly, and even through the growing darkness of the evening they could see the lone leaf still hanging from the branch against the wall. And then, with the coming of the night, the wind began to blow again, and the rain began to fall heavily.

But the next morning, when Johnsy commanded that the curtain be raised again, the leaf was still there.

Johnsy lay for a long time looking at it. And then she called to Sue.

"I've been a bad girl, Sue," said Johnsy. "Something has made that last leaf stay there just to show me how bad I was. It was a sin to want to die. You may bring me a little soup now—and then put some pillows behind me and I will sit up and watch you cook."

An hour later Johnsy said, "Sue, some day I want to paint a picture of the Bay of Naples."

The doctor came in the afternoon. "You are doing fine," he said, taking Johnsy's thin hand in his. "In another week or so you will be perfectly well. And now I must go to see another patient downstairs. His name is Behrman. He is some kind of artist, I believe. Pneumonia, too. He is an old, weak man, and the attack is very severe. There is no hope for him, but I am sending him to the hospital in order to make him more comfortable."

The next day, Sue came to the bed where Johnsy lay. "The doctor tells me that soon you will be perfectly well again," Sue said, putting her arm around Johnsy. Johnsy smiled at her happily.

"Isn't it wonderful?" Sue continued. "But now I have something sad to tell you. Old Mr. Behrman died this morning of pneumonia. They found him two days ago in his room. He was helpless with pain and fever. His shoes and clothing were wet and icy. No one could understand where he had gone on such a terrible night. Then they found a ladder and a lantern which was still lighted. They also found some paint and a brush which was still wet with green paint."

"Do you understand what happened?" Sue asked with tears in her eyes. "During the night—in all that wind and rain—Mr. Behrman climbed up and painted a green leaf on the wall of the house across from us. Didn't you think it was strange that the leaf never moved when the wind blew? Ah, darling, it was Behrman's true masterpiece—he painted it there the night that the last leaf fell."

Comprehension and Discussion

1. Who was Mr. Behrman? How did he make a living?
2. What did he think of Sue and Johnsy?
3. What did Behrman say when Sue told him of Johnsy's idea?
4. What was the weather like during Johnsy's illness?
5. What gave Johnsy the hope to get better?
6. How did Behrman catch pneumonia?
7. What do you think of Behrman's last act (and first painting)?
8. What is pneumonia? How do doctors treat this illness today?
9. Do you know any artists? What kind of art do you enjoy?
10. Are most people as generous as Mr. Behrman? Give some examples.

Exercises

A. Use each of the following terms in a sentence:
pen name, an interesting twist, Bohemian, story (of a building), to make a living, to feel sure, patient, to succeed in making someone feel something, vine, root, port wine, otherwise, fierce, canvas, to pose, model, pillow, branch, to command, sin, severe, icy, ladder, lantern, paint, brush, to climb up, masterpiece.

B. Circle the term on the right that has a SIMILAR meaning to the term on the left.

Example: silly   seldom/sad/weak/(foolish)

1. scarcely   frequently/rapidly/rarely/usually
2. make up one's   hesitate/prefer/decide/refuse
   mind
3. permit   refuse/allow/dare/enjoy

4. perhaps   maybe/always/allow/anyway
5. for instance often/for example/fortunately/forever
6. watchdog   madman/clock/guardian/animal
7. there is no   we're hopeful/hope is everywhere/it
   hope   is always possible/it's useless
8. above   beneath/over/beside/under
9. would rather must/ought to/insist on/prefer
10. resemble   look like/occupy/paint/try

C. Circle the word on the right that RHYMES with the word on the left.

Example: would   gold/good/shoulder/loud

1. sign   lion/line/seen/been
2. knees   niece/peace/sneeze/face
3. comb   come/tomb/thumb/home
4. could   cold/pulled/good/soiled
5. drawer   far/store/near/under
6. climb   limb/dumb/clam/time
7. ache   catch/touch/take/like
8. passed   least/fast/lasted/hissed
9. was   cause/has/does/is
10. mind   kind/send/hand/pinned

D. Change the following sentences first to the past tense and then to the present perfect tense.

Example: They enjoy living among so many artists.
            (They enjoyed living among so many artists.)
            (They have enjoyed living among so many artists.)

1. This adds to the interest of the place.
2. They are living in a three-story building.
3. The artist is visiting the city.
4. She lies on her bed all day.
5. Is she worrying about it?
6. She doesn't want to die.
7. She is feeling very ill.
8. The doctor is leaving.
9. The leaves will fall slowly.
10. He works in his studio all afternoon.

Unit 2: The Stolen Letter

Edgar Allan Poe

During his lifetime, Edgar Allan Poe (1809–1849) was more popular in France than in his native United States. Poe's stories always have an air of psychological mystery or horror.

PART ONE

In Paris, just after dark one evening in the autumn of 18--, I was enjoying the company of an old friend, C. Auguste Dupin, in his small library. The door of the room was opened suddenly and another old friend, Monsieur G., head of the Paris police, entered.

We were glad to see Monsieur G., for we had not seen him for several years. He said that he had come to consult us, or rather to ask the opinion of my friend Dupin, about some official business which was causing him a great deal of trouble.

"I will tell you in a few words what it is," he said, "but before I begin, let me tell you that this is a matter of great secrecy, and I might lose my job if people knew that I had told someone about it."

"Proceed," said I.

"Well, I have received confidential information that a document of great importance has been stolen from the royal apartments. The thief is Minister D. The person from whom the letter was stolen needs it badly. But, of course, he cannot proceed openly. And he has asked me to take care of the problem."

"My first act," he went on, "was to make a careful inspection of the minister's apartment. Of course, I had to do this secretly and without his knowledge because we do not want the minister to know that we suspect him. Fortunately, the daily habits of the minister helped me greatly. He is frequently absent from home at night. He has only a few servants and they do not sleep in his apartment. I have keys, as you know, with which I can open any door in Paris. For three months, I was busy personally searching his apartment. It is now a question of my honor and my reputation. In addition, the reward is enormous. Therefore, I continued to search for a long time. This thief is a very clever man. I searched every corner of his apartment, but I still couldn't find the paper."

"It is possible," I suggested, "that the minister had the letter but has hidden it somewhere outside the apartment."

"Oh, no!" said Monsieur G. "Twice he has been stopped on the street by my own men, pretending to be thieves, and they have searched him carefully."

"Tell us," said I, "exactly what you did in your search of the apartment."

"I have had experience in these matters," answered Monsieur G. "Thus, I examined the apartment room by room, spending an entire week in each room. We examined the furniture. We opened every drawer, and I also looked for secret drawers. Next, we examined the chairs. We removed the tops from all the tables."

"But," I said, "you were not able to take apart all the pieces of furniture. That would be impossible."

"Of course," he answered, "but we did better. We examined every section of each piece of furniture under a very powerful microscope, and we found no indications or marks that the furniture had been touched or disturbed in any way to create a

9

hiding place for the letter. After we had examined the furniture, we examined the apartment itself. We divided the entire surface into sections and gave a number to each section so that we could not possibly miss any. Then we inspected each square inch of the apartment."

"You examined the grounds around the house?"

"Yes, but that was no trouble. The grounds are paved with bricks. We examined each brick, and also the grass between the bricks, and found no indication that anything had been touched or moved."

"You looked among the minister's papers, of course, and into the books of his library?"

"Certainly, we opened every package. We not only opened every book but turned every page. We also inspected the cover of each book with our microscope."

"You examined the floors beneath the carpets?"

"Certainly! We removed every carpet and examined every board beneath the carpets."

"And the paper on the walls?"

"Yes."

"You looked in the cellar?"

"We did."

"Then," I said, "you have been making a mistake, and the letter is not in the apartment."

"I am afraid you are right," said Monsieur G. "And now, Dupin, what would you advise me to do?"

"I would advise you to make a second careful search of the apartment," said Dupin.

"But I am sure the letter is not in the apartment," said Monsieur G.

"I have no better advice to give you," said Dupin. "Of course, you have an accurate description of the letter."

"Oh, yes," said the officer. Then, producing a notebook, he began to read a description of the missing letter. Soon afterward he left, a very unhappy man.

Comprehension

1. What was unusual about Edgar Allan Poe's popularity?
2. Why did Monsieur G. go to visit Dupin?
3. What was stolen? By whom?
4. How did Monsieur G. search the apartment of the man he suspected?

5. Why did he discontinue the search? After how long?
6. Why did the police search the apartment secretly?
7. Why did they stop the minister on the street?
8. What did they do in his library?
9. Why did the search around the grounds give the police little trouble?
10. What was Dupin's advice?

PART TWO

About a month later, Monsieur G. visited us again. We were seated in the library as before.

"Well, what about the missing letter?" I asked him after he sat down. "I suppose you have decided at last that the minister is too clever to be caught."

"Damn it, yes," he said. "I examined the apartment again, as Dupin suggested, but without success."

"How much money has been offered as the reward?" asked Dupin.

"A great deal," he said. "In fact, the amount has been doubled recently. But if it were three times as much, I still couldn't find it. But I will give my personal check for fifty thousand francs to anyone who gets that letter for me."

"In that case," said Dupin, "you can write me a check for that amount. When you have signed the check, I will give you the letter."

Both Monsieur G. and I were greatly surprised. For a moment the officer remained speechless, but then, recovering himself, he picked up a pen and wrote a check for fifty thousand francs and handed it to Dupin. Dupin examined the check carefully and then put it into his pocket. Then he unlocked a drawer and took out a letter and gave it to Monsieur G. It was the stolen letter. The officer accepted it with a trembling hand. He read its contents and then rushed from the room and from the house. When he had gone, Dupin began to explain to me how he had gotten the letter.

"I knew the minister in question very well," he said. "He is a mathematician and a poet—and also a very clever and daring man. I knew that such a man would be familiar with all the usual actions of the police and that he would prepare himself against them. His frequent absences from home at night were only a trick. He knew that the police would search every corner of his apartment, and so he permitted them to do it freely. I saw that he would do something very simple.

"The police, however, never suspected that the minister had placed the letter clearly under the nose of everybody in order to prevent anyone from seeing it.

"With this in mind, I put on a pair of dark glasses and went to visit the minister one fine morning in his apartment. I told him that my eyes were very weak and that, therefore, I had to wear dark glasses. But with my dark glasses I was able to inspect the whole apartment without his noticing the movement of my eyes. Finally, I noticed a small box in full view on the mantelpiece. In this box were five or six visiting cards and a letter. The letter was very dirty and was torn across the middle. It had been put carelessly into one of the sections of the box. As soon as I saw the letter, I was sure it was the one I was looking for. Certainly it was different in appearance from the original letter. The address on the envelope was different; the handwriting on the envelope had also been changed. It looked as if the letter had been written by a woman. But the size was the same. All these things, in the view of every visitor to the apartment, made me suspicious. I examined the letter as carefully as I could without the minister's noticing me, and it was clear to me that the letter had been turned inside out, like a glove, and readdressed and changed slightly. I later said good-bye to the minister but left my cigarette case on the table intentionally.

"The next morning I called upon him again to get my cigarette case. We began to converse again, but suddenly there was a pistol shot in the street. Minister D. rushed to the window and remained there several minutes looking into the street. Actually, it was all part of my plan. One of my own men had fired the shot in order to attract attention. Anyway, while Minister D. was busy at the window, I stepped to the mantelpiece, took the letter, and replaced it with an exact copy which I had prepared at home and brought with me."

"But why did you replace the letter with a copy? Why didn't you take the letter openly on your first visit and leave?"

"Minister D. is a clever and dangerous man," Dupin replied. "There are many men in the house whom he employs. If I had done the foolish thing which you suggest, it is possible I would never have left the place alive and the good people of Paris would never have heard of me again."

Comprehension and Discussion

1. What did the police officer say when he returned a month later?
2. How much was offered as a reward for finding the letter?
3. Describe the manner in which Dupin received the reward.
4. What did he know about the minister?
5. What did Dupin pretend when he went to the minister's house?
6. Where was the stolen letter?
7. How did Dupin distract the minister?
8. Why did Dupin replace the letter with a copy?
9. What qualities does a person need in order to be a good detective like Dupin?
10. How do most detectives investigate crimes?

Exercises

A. Use each of the following terms in a sentence:
psychological, mystery, just after dark, a great deal, confidential, to proceed, honor, reputation, twice, indication, beneath, an accurate description, speechless, mathematician, freely, appearance, under one's nose, mantelpiece, in order to.

B. Fill in the blanks in the following sentences with one of the terms from the list. Change the form if necessary.

to permit	inside out	to be able
in full view of	in addition	to put on
to double	to make a mistake	of course
simple	microscope	

Example: It was cold outside, so before we left the house we ___put on___ our coats.

1. The box was there on the mantelpiece _____ everyone in the room.
2. "Did you search the room?" he asked. " _____ I did," I answered impatiently.
3. He _____ us to search the entire apartment.
4. They _____ the reward from 25,000 to 50,000 francs.
5. If you want to examine the evidence carefully, you may have to look at it under a _____.
6. It's not quite as _____ as you think; it's much more complicated.

7. _____ to the house, we also searched the yard.
8. We turned the room _____ looking for the letter, but we were unable to find it.
9. I think I _____ on my last test; I won't get a perfect score.
10. _____ you _____ to understand the directions? If not, I'll help you.

C. Place the adverb in its normal position in each sentence.

Example: He leaves the key in the drawer. (often)
      (He often leaves the key in the drawer.)

1. I ask for his advice before I do anything. (always)
2. She leaves the house before noon. (seldom)
3. He makes a mistake. (rarely)
4. He gives advice without being asked for it. (never)
5. It rains in the spring in New York. (often)
6. She reads aloud to her children. (hardly ever)
7. She looks out the window before she goes out. (always)
8. He wakes up before the alarm goes off. (rarely)
9. He was able to use that machine properly. (never)
10. I am at work by 9 A.M. (usually)

D. Change the following sentences so that the object of the two-word verb becomes a pronoun.

Example: She cut up the meat.
      (She cut it up.)

1. She took out the cups.
2. He's going to put on his hat.
3. I had to cut off Mrs. Smith before she finished speaking.
4. I asked them to wake up my uncle at five o'clock.
5. I want to take Sally out some night next week.
6. I'm going to take off my sweater when I go in the house.
7. He is getting ready to put away the dishes.
8. She wanted him to try on that suit.
9. She had to cut her hair because it was too long.
10. I put down my book in the living room.

Unit 3: The Celebrated Jumping Frog of Calaveras County

Mark Twain

Mark Twain was the pen name of Samuel Langhorne Clemens (1835–1910). His most famous stories were about Tom Sawyer and Huckleberry Finn, but it was this short story which first made him famous.

PART ONE

Because a friend of mine asked me, I called on good-natured, talkative old Simon Wheeler and asked him about my friend's friend, Leonidas W. Smiley. This story is the result of that visit. I have a deep suspicion that Leonidas W. Smiley doesn't exist; that my friend from the East never knew such a person; and that he made the request of me as a joke. I think he imagined that if I went to Wheeler and asked him about Smiley, then Wheeler would make up a story and bore me to death with some terribly long, exasperating, useless tale. If that was my friend's plan, it succeeded.

I found Simon Wheeler dozing comfortably by the barroom stove of the dilapidated tavern in the decayed mining camp of Angel's, and I noticed that he was fat and baldheaded. He looked gentle, and his face showed him to be a happy, peaceful man. He awakened and greeted me enthusiastically. I told him that a friend of mine had asked me to ask around about an old friend of his from childhood. My friend's old friend was named Leonidas W. Smiley. I further explained that my friend thought that Smiley was a young minister of the Gospel and that he lived in Angel's Camp—or at least he used to. I told Wheeler that I would be very grateful if he could tell me anything about Smiley, since I wanted to honor my friend's request.

Simon Wheeler backed me into a corner and blockaded me there with his chair. He then sat down and proceeded to tell me the most boring, monotonous story I had ever heard. He never smiled, he never frowned, he never changed his voice from the gentle-flowing key which he started with, he never showed the slightest amount of enthusiasm. His story was flat and dull. But, interesting to note, throughout the entire tale he showed himself to be earnest and sincere. It was a wild tale (as you will soon see, since I am going to repeat it word for word), but he never showed me that he thought it wasn't true. It never occurred to him that it was a story either. He regarded it as a truly important matter, and he clearly admired its two heroes as men of taste, wit, and intelligence. I let him tell it in his own way and never interrupted him once. Here is his story:

"Reverend Leonidas W. . . . Hmm, Reverend . . . Well, there was a fellow here once by the name of *Jim* Smiley, but no Leonidas . . . That was back in the winter of 1849—or maybe it was the spring of '50—I don't remember exactly, but what makes me think it was one or the other of those times is that the big flume wasn't finished when he first came to Angel's Camp. But anyway, he was the most curious man you ever saw about betting. He would bet on anything and everything he could, and if he couldn't get anyone to bet on the other side, then he'd change sides. It didn't matter which side he was on, as long as he could bet. If he had a bet on with a person, he was happy; if he didn't, he wasn't satisfied until he did. And the interesting thing is that he was pretty lucky. He almost always won his bets, even when he had changed sides on a bet. He was always waiting and ready for someone to come along so he could offer him some sort of bet. If there was a horse race, he'd bet all he had, and at the end of it he'd either be broke or he'd have a lot of money. If there was a dog fight, he'd bet on it; if there was a cat fight, he'd bet on it; if there was a chicken fight, he'd bet on it; why, if there were two birds sitting on a fence, he'd bet you which one would fly first. Even if he saw a little bug on the ground walking along somewhere, he'd bet you how long it would take the bug to get there (wherever it was the bug was going), and then he'd follow that bug all day to see if he won. Lots of people are still here who remember Jim. They'll tell you what he was like. It never made a bit of difference to him—he'd bet on *anything*. One time the preacher's wife was sick and we all thought she was going to die. A few days later, the preacher came out and told us how the Lord had smiled on his good wife and that she was going to live. Smiley offered to bet him a dollar that she wouldn't.

"Smiley owned a horse while he was here. We used to kid him and call her the fifteen-minute nag because she was so slow, but actually she wasn't too slow, we just liked to kid Jim. He used to win money betting on her. She was sick a lot, so in races the others used to give her a few hundred yards' head start. The other horses would always catch up and pass her, but then near the end of the race, she'd get all excited and desperate and start running faster. She looked silly. She looked as if she were going to fall down with her crazy legs going in all directions and with her coughing and sneezing and almost falling over, but somehow she would pull all of her strength together at the very end and she almost always won by a nose.

"Jim also had a fighting dog which he named after the President, Andrew Jackson. That was the ugliest dog on earth, and he looked as if he were about to die any minute, and when he didn't look that way, he looked as if he wanted to steal something like a common thief. But when the time came to fight another dog, Jim's pup was another dog. At first, Jim's dog appeared ready to lose to the other dog. The other dog would run him around and tackle him, bite him, and throw him all over the ring. People would start to increase their bets against Andrew Jackson. Then, all of a sudden, Jim's pup would come alive. He'd grab the other dog by the hind legs and freeze to them. He wouldn't chew, you understand, he would just hold on until the other dog had to give up.

"Smiley always won money on that dog. Always except once, that is. The dog had to fight another dog, as usual, but this time the other dog had no hind legs. Well, old Andrew Jackson didn't know what to make of it and he lost that fight. Afterwards, he just shook his head, slinked off past Smiley as though he were ashamed of what had happened, and then lay down and died."

Comprehension

1. What was Mark Twain's real name?
2. What did the narrator suspect about his Eastern friend's request?
3. Who were the following: Leonidas W. Smiley, Jim Smiley, and Simon Wheeler?
4. Where did the narrator find Wheeler? What did he look like?
5. What manner did Wheeler use when he told the story?
6. How did Wheeler decide on the time when Smiley was in Angel's Camp?
7. What did he say about Smiley and betting?
8. How did Smiley's horse perform in races?
9. What did Smiley's dog look like? What was its name?
10. How did the dog die?

PART TWO

"Smiley had all kinds of other animals which he used to bet on, too. He had other dogs, chickens, cats, and several others which I can't even remember. One time he caught a frog and decided he would teach it to jump. He worked with that frog for about three months, and you can bet that at the end of that time the frog was a pretty good jumper. Jim would give the little beast a punch and the frog would leap higher than any frog you've ever

18

seen. That frog would whirl around in the air and land on its feet just like a cat. He was also good at catching flies.

"Smiley named his frog Daniel Webster and claimed that all any frog ever wanted was a good education. He trained the frog so well that all he had to say was 'Flies, Daniel, flies!' and quick as a wink that frog would leap off the floor to wherever the fly was, catch it with his tongue, and land back where he started. When he landed, the frog would act as if nothing had happened. He'd just scratch his head with his hind foot as if he did that sort of thing all the time. Daniel Webster's best trick was jumping from a seated position; that is, with no running head start. Whenever there was an opportunity for Daniel to test his jumping, Smiley would try to find someone to bet with. He was proud of that frog and wanted to show him off to people.

"One day a stranger came into town and saw Smiley carrying the box which served as the frog's house. 'What might it be that you've got in the box?' he asked Smiley.

"Smiley sensed a possible bet, so he acted indifferently. 'Oh, it's nothing much,' he answered, 'just a frog.'

" 'Well, what's he good for?' asked the fellow as he looked into the box and observed the ordinary-looking animal.

"Carelessly and easily, Smiley said, 'He's only good for *one* thing in this world; he can outjump any frog in Calaveras County.'

"The fellow took the box and looked hard and long into it again, then he shook his head. 'He doesn't look any different from any other frog I've ever seen. I don't believe he's any better either.'

" 'Maybe that's because you don't understand frogs the way I do,' Smiley said, smiling. 'Maybe you haven't had any experience. Maybe you're just an amateur when it comes to frogs. Anyway, it's my opinion that this frog can beat any frog in the county and I've got forty dollars here that I'll bet against any frog you can put up against mine.'

" 'Well, I'm just a stranger here,' the man said sadly, 'and I don't have a frog, but if I had one, I'd bet you.'

"Smiley smiled slowly. 'That's all right, that's all right. If you just hold my box here for a minute, I'll go and get you a frog.' And that's what happened. The fellow took the box with Daniel Webster in it while Smiley went off to find a suitable opponent for a jumping contest. They both put up forty dollars, winner take all.

"While he was waiting for Smiley to return, the fellow took the frog out of the box and fed him a few teaspoons of whiskey. Of course he didn't tell Smiley that he had done this, and when Smiley returned from the swamp with a good-looking frog to serve as Daniel's opponent, the fellow had put quite a bit of liquor into the little beast.

"Smiley was excited, as he always was when there was a bet. 'Put the two of them next to each other on this line on the floor, and I'll give the word to begin.' Smiley shouted and the two men touched their frogs, but Daniel Webster didn't move. The other frog leaped straight up and then hopped off in a lively manner all the way across the room. Smiley's frog straightened its legs and reached up as though to jump, but then settled back down as though his feet were glued to the floor. Smiley was sad and disgusted, but he had no idea what the matter was.

"The fellow took the money and started to leave, but as he was going out the door, he turned, jerked his thumb at Daniel and said, 'He's not so good. Any old swamp frog can outjump him!'

"Smiley just stood there a long time looking down at his frog and wondering what was wrong with him. 'He looks fat and saggy,' he finally said as he reached down to pick Daniel up. 'Good Lord, he weighs five pounds!' Smiley shouted, and at that moment the frog belched up a couple of ounces of whiskey. When Smiley realized what had happened, he was so mad he could hardly see straight, and he started chasing after the fellow who had won his money, but he never caught him. One other time . . ."

At this moment someone called to Simon from across the street, so he went over to see what the person wanted. "Don't move, stranger," he said to me as he got up from his chair, "I'll only be gone a minute. I want to tell you about another time when Smiley had a yellow, one-eyed cow with no tail, just a short stump that looked like a banana . . ."

I had neither time nor inclination to hear about the afflicted cow, so I waited until Wheeler was halfway across the street, and then I ran out of Angel's Camp as fast as I could.

Comprehension and Discussion

1. What other kinds of animals did Smiley own besides his dog?

2. Who was Daniel Webster? What did Smiley train him to do?
3. What did the stranger say when he saw Daniel's box?
4. Why did Smiley go to the swamp?
5. What did the stranger do while Smiley was at the swamp?
6. What do you think would happen if you gave a small animal some whiskey?
7. Why couldn't Daniel jump? How much did Smiley lose because he couldn't jump?
8. What did Smiley do when he figured out what had happened?
9. Do you like to bet? What kinds of contests or games do people bet on in your area?
10. Why did the narrator of this story wonder if Wheeler's story were true?

Exercises

A. Use each of the following terms in a sentence:
talkative, suspicion, to make up a story, exasperating, to doze, dilapidated, at least, monotonous, sincere, as long as, some sort of, head start, to win by a nose, to give up, that is, to whirl, quick as a wink, to be proud, to belch, ounce, hardly.

B. Match the word in the left column with its OPPOSITE in the right column.

Example: _a_ **4.** suitable   **a.** inappropriate

__ 1. talkative	**a.** inappropriate
__ 2. hind	**b.** unusual
__ 3. freeze	**c.** silent
__ 4. suitable	**d.** calm
__ 5. carelessly	**e.** dull
__ 6. stranger	**f.** standing
__ 7. seated	**g.** boil
__ 8. excited	**h.** front
__ 9. interesting	**i.** carefully
__ 10. ordinary	**j.** friend

C. Change the following sentences to the past perfect tense.

Example: I went to Angel's Camp.
(I had gone to Angel's Camp.)

1. He wrote many famous stories.
2. Smiley won all of his bets.
3. We saw the one-eyed cow.
4. He catches flies with his tongue.
5. Did you make a request?
6. He didn't drink any liquor.
7. We have always bet on horse races.
8. He was dozing comfortably.
9. He bet on one and then he changed sides.
10. She followed them all day.

D. Give the noun form of the following adjectives.

   Example: comfortable ___comfort___

   1. enthusiastic _____
   2. peaceful _____
   3. sincere _____
   4. important _____
   5. curious _____
   6. different _____
   7. desperate _____
   8. easy _____
   9. sad _____
   10. suspicious _____

Unit 4: The Wreck of the *Commodore*

Newspaper accounts from the
Florida Times-Union
and *The New York Press*

These are actual newspaper articles about the sinking of a ship and the adventures of Stephen Crane, the famous American writer who was on that ship. Crane was world-renowned for his novel The Red Badge of Courage. *The dateline of the series, which ran over a three-day period, is Jacksonville, Florida, 1897.*

PART ONE

THE COMMODORE SINKS AT SEA

The Little Vessel Lost with Her Cargo and Ammunition

THE STEAMER *COMMODORE*, which left here Thursday night with an expedition of Cuban freedom fighters, is now resting on the bottom of the sea, twenty fathoms[1] below the surface, about eighteen miles northeast of Mosquito Inlet.

All of the twenty-eight men on the vessel reached the shore safely, and twelve of them arrived in Jacksonville last night on the Florida East Coast Railway. The other sixteen are still down the coast but are expected to arrive here on a special train this morning.

Details of the Accident

From the accounts given by the men in the boat, the following details of the accident were learned. The *Commodore* crossed the St. Johns bar[2] at two o'clock Friday afternoon while the sea was very high. As she was crossing the bar, she got in the trough[3] of the sea and came very near being swamped.

About twelve o'clock Friday night, it was discovered that the boat was leaking badly. The swash[4] of the water as the vessel rolled from side to side soon alarmed everyone on board. Captain Murphy, Stephen Crane, R. A. Delgado, and one or two others quieted the excitement and put everybody to work on the pumps with buckets. The steam pump was started and for two hours the water was poured over the sides in streams. The men worked hard and in the meantime, the steamer's bow turned west. She was making good time toward the shore, which was at least forty miles away. The steamer was headed due east after leaving the bar, as she wished to keep out of the way of the cruiser *Newark*.

At two-thirty A.M., the water was steadily rising, so they decided to abandon the vessel.

In the Boats

Paul Rojo; R. A. Delgado; Franco Blanco, the old Cuban pilot; and nine other men took one of the boats and left the steamer. Captain Murphy, the first and second mate, the engineer and assistant, Stephen Crane, and ten other men took the

---

1. *fathom:* six feet, a measurement used for the sea   2. *bar:* an offshore hill of sand   3. *trough:* a long, narrow depression between waves   4. *swash:* the splash of liquid

large yawl,[5] and at three o'clock they left the *Commodore* to her fate. The night was dark and they could not see what happened, but they think that the boat and all the guns sank to the bottom of the sea.

STEPHEN CRANE, NOVELIST, SWIMS ASHORE
Young New York Writer Astonishes the Sea Dogs by His Courage in the Face of Death

JACKSONVILLE, FLA., Jan. 3—Seventeen men are accounted for out of the twenty-eight on the Cuban steamer *Commodore*. There is a chance that seven more are alive. Five men came ashore at Daytona this noon: Captain Murphy; Stephen Crane, the novelist; the cook; and two sailors. One of them, Higgins of Rhode Island, died soon after reaching land because of severe wounds received while landing. His family lives in Boston. One of the survivors gives the following details:

Story of a Survivor

"The tug[6] sank at seven o'clock Saturday morning, twenty miles off New Smyrna, and the Americans on board remained till the last moment. The leak was discovered at about three o'clock A.M. The pumps would not work long, though they did good service for a while.

"When the captain saw the water still rising, he turned the ship toward shore, but she continued to sink. Twelve men were first sent off. One boat containing six men capsized, and I am afraid that the men were lost. The Americans all remained on the tug till she sank. One raft was made up from materials thrown to them, and they then disappeared from our sight. Captain Murphy; Stephen Crane, the novelist and correspondent; Higgins; myself; and one other sailor left at the last moment. We tried to save the men in the water around us, but the heavy seas and blinding wind swept them away. The spray was so thick that we could see only a few rods.[7] We could do nothing. It was difficult to keep our small boat right side up."

Thrown into the Breakers

"For twenty-four hours we battled with the heavy seas, constantly bailing, and at last sighted land. As we attempted to

---

5. *yawl:* a ship's small boat   6. *tug:* a powerful small boat designed to tow large vessels   7. *rod:* a unit of measurement equal to five meters

land, the wind drove us, and all of a sudden the boat overturned and we were struggling for life. For an hour we battled for life, and then we managed to crawl out of the sands, almost dead. Captain Murphy saved Mr. Crane by helping him when he got tired. Higgins was struck on the head by floating timbers and he died soon after landing. He was a good sailor and a brave man. He worked to save his comrades."

PRAISE FOR CRANE

DAYTONA, FLA., Jan. 3—"That newspaperman was brave," said the cook of the *Commodore* tonight in reference to Stephen Crane, the novelist, who was after material for stories. "He didn't seem to know what fear was. He was listed on the ship's papers as an able seaman[8] at twenty dollars a month. When we started out, he insisted upon doing a seaman's work, and he did it well, too. When Saturday morning and the troubles came, he came on deck and knew that the vessel was sinking and that it was only a question of time when we would be at the mercy of the terrible sea.

"He stood on the bridge looking out at the horizon in an effort to see land. Once he climbed the rigging to get a better view. I was sure that he would be swept off as the vessel rolled from side to side, almost touching the water as she rolled down.

"When the boats were launched, Crane was the last one, except Captain Murphy, to get in, and his courage helped all of us. In the small dinghy, he rowed as well as the others, even though he was so worn out that he could hardly hold his oar straight in the terrific seas. At the last moment he stood up and, seeing the big wave coming that overthrew us, cried out, 'Look out, boys, there's trouble for us. Jump, Captain!' "

Saves a Drowning Man

"Both he and Captain Murphy were thrown out on the same side. Crane was partially thrown under the overturned boat, but Captain Murphy saved him. We all battled there in the water for hours. Crane was a good swimmer, and he saved one of the sailors, as the man could not swim. Crane had to keep him up with an oar. These newspapermen are good even if they do tell such awful lies at times," concluded the cook, as he took another

8. *able seaman:* a worker on a ship who is certified for all duties

big drink of the "life preservative" provided by the good people here . . .

Comprehension
1. Where did these reports first appear? When?
2. What kind of ship was the *Commodore?* Where is it now?
3. When did the ship leave port? How long was it at sea when the trouble began?
4. What happened at two-thirty A.M.? At three o'clock?
5. What is a yawl? A dinghy?
6. Who went ashore at Daytona on January 3?
7. What did Stephen Crane do for a living?
8. Why was he on board?
9. What work did he do on board?
10. How did Crane save a drowning man?

PART TWO

STEPHEN CRANE, the writer, is safe, and readers of *The Press* may expect in a short time a treat from his wonderful pen.

Mr. Crane was on the way to Cuba to write about the war there. He will get to Cuba as soon as he can. He was frightened by the experience in the lifeboat. His letters will appear in *The Press* as soon as they arrive.

Mr. Crane has not told us what he is going to write; probably he does not know himself. But we know that his reports will be as interesting as his stories, *The Red Badge of Courage, The Third Violet, George's Mother,* and *Maggie: A Girl of the Streets.*

Experience as a Reporter

Stephen Crane has been famous in New York more than any writer lately. He was a New York reporter at the age of sixteen. In his newspaper work he didn't like working with facts, so he took to writing stories.

New York was happier then than now. Its lights and shadows attracted him. There he found all the human emotions. He listened and studied. His stories had as their background the slums and the palaces. They were very realistic. His English flowed simple and pure like a clean river.

His Genius Recognized

He was only a boy, but everyone loved his work. The old novelists found his war scenes so vivid that they could scarcely believe they were painted by one who never had smelled gunpowder except at a shooting match . . .

Story of the Wreck of the *Commodore* Told by the Commander

CAPTAIN MURPHY's story:

"The engineer reported to me about midnight that the vessel was gaining water in her hold[9] and that he couldn't get the pumps to work. They had tried to get the water out, but the pumps stopped. The pipe was evidently broken. If the water is allowed to get up into the coal, the coal gets wet and chokes the pumps. All the water that entered the ship was in the engine room."

"Was it treachery, do you think?" asked the *Times-Union* reporter.

"No, I don't think so. It was neglect, more than anything else."

"I gave the order to use the buckets; also an order to throw everything into the furnace, hoping to get up steam to run into Mosquito Inlet, about eighteen miles west of us. The men worked hard. None stood back, but the water rose slowly and we had not gone three miles when the fires went out. There was no hope of saving the ship. I told the men to go to the boats. We got two of the boats off with all the Cubans.

"One boat had Julio Rodriguez Baz, and those with him were Manuel Gonzalez, Luis Sierra Mederos, and Jesus Alvarez. . . . Señor Baz's boat stood near us so they could help us, but we told them to go ahead. Later on we launched the ship's boat, with seven men, including Mate Crane. I told all those to go who wanted to. All went except Mr. Crane, a brave little gentleman, Steward Montgomery, and William Higgins. I wanted to stay with the ship and then put ashore in the dinghy. Later on we also left."

One Boat Stove In

"We had proceeded a few yards when we heard a cry from the ship: 'The big boat is stove!'[10] They were also flying a distress flag."

"I don't know how this happened, unless the mate returned and attempted to get something he had forgotten. We immedi-

9. *hold:* the part of a ship where cargo is stored 10. *stove* (present tense *stave*): to break or smash a hole in

ately went back and I told the men to build a raft; they made three. Meanwhile, our little boat was remaining distant about two hundred yards.

"Finally, they begged us to take them in tow. We made a towline, but the sea nearly filled our boat, so we let go. We went back again, but the sea broke our towline. The rafts were scattered. I told the men to return to the vessel and make another raft while I bailed out. Then, fifty yards away, the big ship sank. Three men went down with her, like heroes, with no cry, not a sound. I stayed by the rafts twenty minutes longer, but the wind was strong, so we allowed our boat to go wherever the wind carried us."

How They Landed

"Saturday afternoon at four o'clock, we saw the coast north of Mosquito Inlet. We saw people on shore, so I fired my pistol to attract their attention. I know that they saw us and our perilous position, for we were only a half mile from shore. Feeling certain that we had been seen, and thinking that they would send us a sturdy boat, we waited at the spot, pulling hard against the heavy sea and wind all that afternoon and all that night. I do not see now, looking back upon it, how we thought we could do it. The wind was too strong. The next morning we found ourselves off the beach of Daytona, and seeing no one, made one last desperate effort with our remaining strength to reach shore. I gave one life belt to the steward and one to Mr. Crane." [The captain does not say that he had a badly injured arm and shoulder.] "The sea upset the boat and washed us all away. I grabbed the boat and got on the bottom, but she rolled over again. Higgins tried to swim but sank. I tried to encourage him, and he made another attempt. The boat went over again, and I saw no more of him until his corpse came up on the beach."

Death of Higgins

"John Getchell, who lives near the beach, saw that we were in trouble. He got into the water and helped the steward and Mr. Crane in. I was safe in shallow water. I then saw Higgins' body on the wet sand. We rolled him and made every effort to save him but unfortunately failed. Poor fellow, he was brave and did his duty faithfully.

"We had not been on the beach long before the good women of the town came to us with hot coffee. They were very kind. Not one of these women came to us without some present of

29

food, clothing, or shelter. The people of Daytona buried poor Higgins at their own expense."

Captain Murphy had his arm in a sling but otherwise seemed all right. All of the men looked tired and worn out.

Crane's Splendid Grit

"That man Crane is wonderful," said Captain Murphy tonight to a *Press* correspondent in speaking of the wreck. "The sea was so rough that even old sailors got seasick, but Crane behaved like a born sailor. He and I were about the only ones not affected by the big seas which tossed us about. As we went south he sat in the pilothouse with me, smoking and talking. When the leak was discovered, he was the first man to volunteer aid."

Jokes Amid Danger

"His shoes, new ones, were slippery on the deck, and he took them off and tossed them overboard, saying, with a laugh: 'Well, Captain, I guess I won't need them if we have to swim.' He stood on the deck by me all the while and helped me direct the escape from the dying ship. He even took his turn at the oars."

Tries to Save Higgins

"When we went over, I called to him to see that he was all right and he replied that he would obey orders. He was under the boat once, but got out in some way. He held up Higgins when the man got so tired and tried to bring him in, but the sailor was so far gone that he was almost dead. When we were thrown up onto the waves, Crane was the first man to stagger up the beach looking for houses. He's a brave man with plenty of grit," concluded the captain.

Comprehension and Discussion

1. What did Crane do when he was sixteen? How did others view him?
2. Why did he go to live in New York City?
3. What did Captain Murphy say had happened to the pumps?
4. What happened after the fires went out?
5. Why couldn't the men on the boat tow the rafts?
6. Who was John Getchell? What did he do?
7. What did the people on shore at Daytona do?
8. How did Crane behave during the crisis?

30

9. What can you say about the language used in these old reports?
10. What kind of person do you think Stephen Crane was?

Exercises

A. Use each of the following terms in a sentence:
to be accounted for, correspondent, slum, aid, overboard, grit, partially, to row, timbers, to float, ill-fated, to be only a question of time, surf, to deal with someone severely, to embark, distress, raft, versatile, recent years, literary circles.

B. Fill in the blanks in the following sentences with one of the terms from the list. Change the form if necessary.

expedition	fathom	mate
survivor	capsize	floating
vessel	perilous	corpse
chagrin	deck	

Example: The waves were so high that our boat __capsized__ and then sank.

1. We don't know how far down it is to the bottom of the sea, but we think it's about sixteen _____.
2. There were several pieces of timber _____ on top of the sea around the wreck of the ship.
3. Stephen Crane was one of the _____ of the wreck of the *Commodore*.
4. We realized that we were in a _____ situation when the waves began to turn us over.
5. The _____ which sank off Florida was called the *Commodore*.
6. Higgins drowned during the storm, but we didn't know this until his _____ washed ashore.
7. The _____ of Cubans was bound for the island in order to mount a military action.
8. The men bailed water with all of their strength, but much to their _____, the water level in the boat continued to get higher.
9. The worker who is second in command after the captain of a ship is the second _____.
10. He stood on the _____ of the steamer and watched the storm.

31

C. Fill in the blanks in the following sentences with the correct form of the verb in parentheses.

Example: Crane wanted _____ (go) to Cuba on a ship.

(Crane wanted to go to Cuba on a ship.)

1. In the dinghy, Crane _____ (row) as well as any man.
2. How did this _____ (happen)?
3. Three men _____ (go) down with the ship when it sank.
4. If they find the traitor, they _____ (deal) with him severely.
5. We tried _____ (reach) the shore by rowing.
6. The steamer _____ (want) to keep out of the way of the *Newark,* so it _____ (sail) east in a hurry.
7. He didn't seem to know what fear _____ (be).
8. I'm afraid to sail because I _____ (know) how to swim.
9. _____ you _____ (leave) Jacksonville yesterday?
10. We tried _____ (get) the pumps _____ (work).

D. Write the plural forms of these words.

Example: hand ___hands___

1. leaf _____
2. half _____
3. wave _____
4. story _____
5. cruiser _____
6. article _____
7. vessel _____
8. hero _____
9. watch _____
10. rescue _____

32

Unit 5: Van Bibber's Burglar

Richard Harding Davis

Richard Harding Davis (1864–1916) was another turn-of-the-century short story writer who also made a living as a reporter. He wrote with a wry humor about sports and big-city living.

PART ONE

There had been a dance uptown, but Van Bibber couldn't go, so he accepted Travers' suggestion that they go over to Jersey City to see a "go" (which was an illegal prize fight without gloves) between a fighter named "Dutchy" Mack and a man who called himself the Black Diamond. They hid the wealth of their clothes by wearing heavy overcoats.

Travers and Van Bibber filled their pockets with cigars, and they also fastened their watches to both key chains. Alf Alpin, who was in charge, was pleased and flattered that they came and insisted that they sit on the platform. It was even whispered that

33

they were the "parties" who were putting up the money to back the Black Diamond against "Hester Street" Jackson. This in itself entitled them to respect. Van Bibber was asked to hold the watch, but he wisely declined. Andy Spielman, the sporting reporter of the *Track and Ring,* whose watchcase was covered with diamonds, was asked to keep time.

It was two o'clock when the fight ended and three before they reached the city. They had another reporter in the cab with them besides the gentleman who had held the watch; and as Van Bibber was very hungry, and as he doubted that he could get anything at that hour at the club, they accepted Spielman's invitation and went for a steak and onions at the Owl's Nest, Gus McGowan's all-night restaurant on Third Avenue.

It was a very dingy, dirty place, but it was as warm as the engine room of a steamboat, and the steak was perfectly done and tender. It was too late to go to bed, so they sat around the table, with their chairs tipped back and their knees against its edge. The two club men had thrown off their coats, and their wide shirt fronts and silk facings shone grandly in the smoky light of the oil lamps and the red glow from the grill in the corner. They talked about the life the reporters led, and the rich men asked foolish questions, which the reporters answered without indicating how foolish they thought the men were.

"And I suppose you have all sorts of curious adventures," said Van Bibber, tentatively.

"Well, no, not what I would call adventures," said one of the reporters. "I have never seen anything that could not be explained or attributed directly to some known cause, such as crime or poverty or drink. You may think at first that you have stumbled on something strange and romantic, but it comes to nothing. You would suppose that in a great city like this one would come across something that could not be explained away —something mysterious. But I have not found it so. Dickens once told James Payn that the most curious thing he ever saw in his rambles around London was a ragged man who stood crouching under the window of a great house where the owner was giving a party. While the man hid beneath a window on the ground floor, a woman, wonderfully dressed and very beautiful, raised the sash from the inside and dropped her bouquet down into the man's hand, and he nodded and stuck it under his coat and ran off with it.

"I call that, now, a really curious thing to see. But I have never come across anything like it, and I have been in every part of this big city, and at every hour of the night and morning. I am not lacking in imagination, but no captured maidens have ever waved to me from barred windows. It is all commonplace and vulgar, and always ends in a dull story."

McGowan, who had fallen asleep behind the bar, woke suddenly and shivered and rubbed his shirt-sleeves briskly. A woman knocked at the side door and asked for food. The man who tended the grill told her to go away. They heard her feeling her way against the wall and cursing as she staggered out of the alley. Three men came in and wanted everybody to drink with them, and they became insolent when the gentlemen declined.

"You see," said the reporter, "it is all like this. Night in a great city is not picturesque and it is not theatrical. It is sodden, sometimes brutal and exciting. It is dramatic, but the plot is old and the motives and characters always the same."

The rumble of heavy market wagons and the rattle of milk carts told them that it was morning, and as they opened the door the cold fresh air swept into the place and made them wrap their collars around their throats. The morning wind swept down the cross street from the East River, and the lights of the street lamps and of the saloon looked old and tawdry. Travers and the reporters went off to a Turkish bath, and the gentleman who held the watch, who had been asleep for the last hour, went home in a taxi. It was almost clear now and very cold. Van Bibber had the strange feeling one gets when one stays up until the sun rises of having lost a day somewhere, and the fight in Jersey City was far back in the past.

The houses along the cross street were dead as so many blank walls, and only here and there a lace curtain waved out of the open window where some honest citizen was sleeping. The street was deserted; not even a cat or a policeman moved on it, and Van Bibber's footsteps sounded brisk on the sidewalk. There was a great house at the corner of the avenue on which he was walking. The house faced the avenue and a stone wall ran back to the brownstone stable which opened on the side street. There was a door in this wall, and as Van Bibber approached it, it opened cautiously, and a man's head appeared in it for an instant and was withdrawn again like a flash, and the door slammed shut. Van Bibber stopped and looked at the door and at the house and up and down the street. The house was tightly closed, and the streets were still empty.

Van Bibber knew he wouldn't frighten an honest man, so he decided the face he had seen must belong to a dishonest one. It was none of his business, he assured himself, but it was curious, and he liked adventure, and he would have liked to prove his reporter friend wrong. So he approached the door silently, then jumped and caught onto the top of the wall and stuck one foot on the handle of the door, and, with the other on the knocker, drew himself up and looked cautiously down on the other side. He had done this so lightly that the only noise he made was the rattle of the doorknob on which his foot had rested, and the man inside thought that the one outside was trying to open the door, and placed his shoulder to it and pressed against it. Van Bibber looked down directly on the other's head and shoulders. He could see the top of the man's head only two feet below, and he also saw that in one hand he held a revolver and that two bags filled with articles of different sizes lay at his feet.

Comprehension

1. Where did Van Bibber go instead of the dance uptown?
2. How were the two wealthy men treated by Alf Alpin?
3. Where did the men go after the fight? Why?
4. What did the men talk about at the restaurant?
5. What do you know about the food and the atmosphere at the restaurant?
6. What was the story that Dickens told to James Payn?
7. What happened when three other men came into the restaurant?
8. Where did the men go in the morning? How did they know it was morning?
9. What happened while Van Bibber was walking?
10. What did he discover when he looked over the wall?

PART TWO

Van Bibber knew that the man below had robbed the big house on the corner and that if it had not been for his having passed when he did, the burglar would have escaped with his treasure. His first thought was that he was not a policeman and that a fight with a burglar was not in his line of life; but this was followed by the thought that though the gentleman who owned the property was of no interest to him, he was, as a respectable member of society, more entitled to consideration than the man with the revolver.

The fact that he was now, whether he liked it or not, perched on the top of the wall like Humpty Dumpty, and that the burglar might see him and shoot him the next minute, also had an immediate influence on his movements. So he balanced himself cautiously and noiselessly and dropped upon the man's head and shoulders, bringing him down with him and under him. The revolver went off once in the struggle, but in an instant Van Bibber was standing up over the man and kicked the pistol out of his fingers. Then he picked it up and said, "Now, if you try to get up, I'll shoot at you." He almost said, "And I'll probably miss you," but subdued it. The burglar, much to Van Bibber's astonishment, did not attempt to rise, but sat up with his hands locked across his knees and said: "Shoot then. I'd rather you would."

His face was bitter and hopeless.

"Go ahead, I won't move. Shoot me."

It was a very unpleasant situation. Van Bibber put the gun down and asked the burglar to tell him all about it.

"You haven't got much heart," said Van Bibber, finally. "You're a pretty poor sort of a burglar, I think."

"What's the use?" said the man. "I won't go back—I won't go back there alive. I've served my time forever in that hole. If I have to go back again, I'll never survive. I'll die if I go back there, I tell you!"

"Go back where?" asked Van Bibber, gently, and greatly interested. "To prison?"

"To prison, yes!" cried the man, hoarsely. "To a grave. That's where. Look at my face," he said, "and look at my hair. That ought to tell you where I've been. With all the color gone out of my skin, and all the life out of my legs. You needn't be afraid of me. I couldn't hurt you if I wanted to. I'm a skeleton and a baby. I couldn't kill a cat. And now you're going to send me back again for another lifetime. For twenty years, this time, into that cold, awful hole."

Van Bibber shifted the pistol from one hand to the other and eyed his prisoner doubtfully.

"How long have you been out?" he asked, seating himself on

37

the steps of the kitchen and holding the revolver between his knees. The sun was driving the morning mist away, and he had forgotten the cold.

"I got out yesterday," said the man.

Van Bibber glanced at the bags and lifted the revolver. "You didn't waste much time," he said.

"No," answered the man, sullenly, "no, I didn't. I knew this place and I wanted money to get West to my folks, and the Society said I'd have to wait until I earned it, and I couldn't wait. I haven't seen my wife or daughter for seven years. Seven years, young man; think of that—seven years. Do you know how long that is? Seven years without seeing your wife or your child! And they're straight people, they are," he added hastily. "My wife moved West after I was put away and took another name, and my girl never knew about me. She thinks I'm away at sea. I was to join them. That was the plan. I was to join them, and I thought I could lift enough here to get the fare, and now," he added, dropping his face in his hands, "I've got to go back. And I had meant to live straight after I got West—God help me, but I did! Not that it makes much difference now. And I don't care whether you believe it or not neither," he added, fiercely.

"I didn't say whether I believed it or not," answered Van Bibber, with grave consideration.

He eyed the man for a brief space without speaking, and the burglar looked back at him, defiantly and with no hope in his eyes. Perhaps it was because of this fact, or perhaps it was the wife and child that moved Van Bibber, but whatever his motives were, he acted on them promptly. "I suppose, though," he said, as though speaking to himself, "that I ought to give you up."

"I'll never go back alive," said the burglar, quietly.

"Well, that's bad, too," said Van Bibber. "Of course, I don't know whether you're lying or not, and as to your meaning to live honestly, I very much doubt it; but I'll give you a ticket to wherever your wife is, and I'll see you on the train. And you can get off at the next station and rob my house tomorrow night, if you feel that way about it. Throw those bags inside that door where the servant will see them before the milkman does, and walk on out ahead of me, and keep your hands in your pockets, and don't try to run. I have your pistol, you know."

The man placed the bags inside the kitchen door, and, with a doubtful look at his custodian, stepped out into the street and walked toward Grand Central Station. Van Bibber kept just behind him, and kept turning the question over in his mind as to what he ought to do. He felt very guilty as he passed each policeman, but he recovered himself when he thought of the wife and child who lived in the West and who were "straight."

"Where to?" asked Van Bibber, as he stood at the ticket-office window. "Helena, Montana," answered the man with, for the first time, a look of relief. Van Bibber bought the ticket and handed it to the burglar. "I suppose you know," he said, "that you can sell that at a place downtown for half the money."

"Yes, I know that," said the burglar.

There was a half hour before the train left, and Van Bibber took the man into the restaurant and watched him eat everything placed before him. Then Van Bibber gave him some money and told him to write to him, and shook hands with him. The man nodded eagerly and pulled off his hat as the car drew out of the station, and Van Bibber went downtown, still wondering if he had done the right thing.

He went to his rooms and changed his clothes, took a cold bath, and crossed over to Delmonico's for his breakfast. He was one of the few customers there; most of the waiters were just beginning to set up for the morning trade. He relaxed and looked over the headlines of the morning newspaper. At first, he leisurely scanned the stories, but then he noticed that an account of the dance listed him as being in attendance. With greater interest he read of the fight between "Dutchy" Mack and the Black Diamond, and then he read carefully how "Abe" Hubbard, alias "Jimmie the Gent," a burglar, had broken jail in New Jersey and had been traced to New York. There was a description of the man, and Van Bibber breathed quickly as he read it. "The detectives have a clue to his whereabouts," the account said, "if he is still in the city they are confident of recapturing him. But they fear that the same friends who helped him to break jail will probably assist him from the country or to get out West."

"They may do that," murmured Van Bibber to himself, with a smile of grim contentment. "They probably will."

Then he said to the waiter, "Oh, I don't know. Some bacon and eggs, orange juice, toast, and coffee."

Comprehension and Discussion

1. What were Van Bibber's first thoughts after he realized that he had found a burglar?

2. What happened when Van Bibber jumped down from the wall?

3. How did the burglar respond to being caught?

4. Where didn't he want to go back to? Why?

5. Where were the two men holding their conversation? What was unusual about that?

6. Why did the burglar want to move West?

7. What did Van Bibber decide to do with the man? Why did he decide that?

8. What would you have decided if you had been Van Bibber? Why?

9. Who was Jimmy the Gent? How did Van Bibber find this out?

10. Do you think any of this really happened? Why?

Exercises

A. Use each of these terms in a sentence:
wry humor, shirt-sleeves, Turkish bath, briskly, doorknob, hopeless, to serve one's time, hastily, God help me, to waste time, respectable, to reiterate, unwarranted, description, to murmur, grim, stable, projecting, patent leather boots.

B. Fill in the blanks in the following sentences with one of the prepositions from the list.

after	beneath	in	under
against	between	on	with
behind	by	through	

Example: ___After___ he left the train station, he went home.

1. He saw a man crouching _____ the window of a house.

2. He knocked the man to the ground and stood with the man's hand _____ his foot.

3. He sat on the steps holding the revolver _____ his knees.

4. He placed his shoulder to the door and pressed _____ it heavily.

5. Travers suggested that Van Bibber go _____ him to a "go."

6. They drove _____ a rough part of town.

7. This morning we came to work _____ bus.

40

8. I hid the book _____ me so that they couldn't see it.
9. If he is still _____ the city, we'll find him.
10. He didn't stand _____ the top of the wall for a long time.

C. Match the word in the right column with its definition in the left column.

Example: ⊥ 8. place of confinement   **j.** jail

___ 1. unusual, interesting   **a.** dingy
___ 2. a handgun   **b.** rattle
___ 3. signal or summon   **c.** burglar
___ 4. dry, ironic   **d.** contentment
___ 5. dark, drab, shabby   **e.** wry
___ 6. short, sharp sounds   **f.** beckon
___ 7. sticking out   **g.** curious
___ 8. place of confinement   **h.** projecting
___ 9. robber of houses   **i.** revolver
___ 10. satisfaction with things as **j.** jail
       they are

D. Rewrite the following sentences using contractions wherever possible.

Example: He was not at the dance last night.
            (He wasn't at the dance last night.)

1. I will never go back alive.
2. She thinks that I am away at sea.
3. I do not know what I want for breakfast.
4. Go ahead. I will not move.
5. We should have called before we came.
6. They could not find anyplace open for breakfast.
7. It did not take long to get there.
8. I would appreciate your assistance.
9. He is the one with the overcoat; she is the one with the gun.
10. You were not at the dance last night.

Unit 6: The Necklace

Guy de Maupassant

Guy de Maupassant (1850–1893) was one of France's best short story writers. He wrote over three hundred in his lifetime and was one of the wealthiest and most famous men of his time.

PART ONE

She was one of those pretty and charming girls who are sometimes, as if by a mistake of destiny, born into a family of clerks. She had no dowry, no expectations, no means of being known, understood, loved, or wedded by any rich and distinguished man; and she let herself be married to a little clerk at the Ministry of Public Instruction.

She dressed plainly because she could not dress well, but her unhappiness seemed to be deeper than one might expect. She seemed to feel that she had fallen from her proper station in life as a woman of wealth, beauty, grace, and charm. She valued these above all else in life, yet she could not attain them. She cared nothing for caste or rank but only for a natural fineness, an instinct for what is elegant, and a suppleness of wit. These would have made her the equal of the greatest ladies of the land. If only she could attain them . . .

She suffered, feeling born for all the delicacies and all the luxuries. She suffered from the poverty of her dwelling, from the wretched look of the walls, from the worn-out chairs, from the ugliness of the curtains. All those things, of which another woman of her rank would never even have been conscious, tortured her and made her angry. The sight of the little Breton peasant who did her humble housework aroused in her despairing regrets and distracted dreams. She thought of silent antechambers hung with Oriental tapestry, lit by tall bronze candelabra, and of two great footmen in knee breeches sleeping in big armchairs, made drowsy by the heavy warmth of the hot-air stove. She thought of long *salons* fitted up with ancient silk, of delicate furniture carrying priceless curiosities, and of coquettish perfumed boudoirs made for talks at five o'clock with intimate friends, with men famous and sought after, whom all women envy and whose attention they all desire.

When she sat down to dinner before the round table covered with a tablecloth three days old, opposite her husband, who uncovered the soup tureen and declared with an enchanted air, "Ah, the good *pot-au-feu!* I don't know anything better than that," she thought of dainty dinners, of shining silverware, of tapestry which peopled the walls with ancient personages and with strange birds flying in the midst of a fairy forest; and she thought of delicious dishes served on marvelous plates, and of the whispered gallantries which you listen to with a sphinxlike smile while you are eating the pink flesh of a trout or the wings of a quail.

She had no dresses, no jewels, nothing. And she loved nothing but that; she felt made for that. She would have liked to be envied, to be charming, to be sought after.

She had a friend, a former schoolmate at the convent, who was rich, and whom she did not like to go and see anymore because she suffered so much when she came back.

But one evening, her husband returned home with a triumphant air and holding a large envelope in his hand.

"There," said he. "Here is something for you."

She tore the paper sharply and drew out a printed card which bore these words:

"The Minister of Public Instruction and Madame Georges Ramponneau request the honor of Monsieur and Madame Loisel's company at the palace of the Ministry on Monday evening, January eighteenth."

Instead of being delighted, as her husband hoped, she threw the invitation on the table with disdain, murmuring, "What do you want me to do with that?"

"But, my dear, I thought you would be glad. You never go out, and this is such a fine opportunity. Everyone wants to go; it is very select, and they are not giving many invitations to clerks. The whole official world will be there."

She looked at him with an irritated glance and said, impatiently, "And what do you want me to put on my back?"

He had not thought of that; he stammered, "Why, the dress you go to the theater in. It looks very well to me."

He stopped, distracted, seeing his wife was crying. Two great tears descended slowly from the corners of her eyes toward the corners of her mouth. He stuttered, "What's the matter? What's the matter?"

But by violent effort she had conquered her grief, and she replied with a calm voice while she wiped her wet cheeks, "Nothing. Only I have no dress and therefore I can't go to this ball. Give your card to some colleague whose wife is better equipped than I."

He was in despair. He resumed, "Come, let us see, Mathilde. How much would it cost, a suitable dress which you could use on other occasions, something very simple?"

She reflected several seconds, making her calculations and wondering also what sum she could ask without drawing on herself an immediate refusal and a frightened exclamation from the economical clerk.

Finally, she replied, hesitatingly, "I don't know exactly, but I think I could manage it with four hundred francs."

He had grown a little pale, because he was laying aside just that amount to buy a gun and treat himself to a little shooting next summer on the plain of Nanterre with several friends who went to shoot larks down there.

But he said, "All right. I will give you four hundred francs. And try to have a pretty dress."

The day of the ball drew near and Mme. Loisel seemed sad, uneasy, and anxious. Her dress was ready, however. Her husband said to her one evening, "What is the matter? Come, you've been so strange these last three days."

And she answered, "It annoys me not to have a single jewel, not a single stone, nothing to put on. I will look like distress. I would almost rather not go at all."

He resumed, "You might wear natural flowers. It's very stylish at this time of the year. For ten francs you can get two or three magnificent roses."

She was not convinced.

"No; there's nothing more humiliating than to look poor among other women who are rich."

But her husband cried, "How stupid you are! Go look up your friend Mme. Forestier and ask her to lend you some jewels. You're a close friend of hers."

She uttered a cry of joy. "It's true! I never thought of it."

The next day she went to her friend and told of her distress. Mme. Forestier went to a wardrobe with a glass door, took out a large jewel box, brought it back, opened it, and said to Mme. Loisel, "Choose, my dear."

She saw first of all some bracelets, then a pearl necklace, and then a Venetian cross, with gold and precious stones of admirable workmanship. She tried on the ornaments before the glass, hesitated, and could not make up her mind to depart with them or to give them back. She kept asking, "Haven't you any more?"

"Why, yes. Look. I don't know what you like."

All of a sudden she discovered in a black satin box a superb necklace of diamonds, and her heart began to beat with an immoderate desire. Her hands trembled as she took it. She fastened it around her throat, outside her high-necked dress, and remained lost in ecstasy at the sight of herself.

Then she asked, hesitating, filled with anguish, "Can you lend me that, only that?"

"Why, yes, certainly."

She sprang upon the neck of her friend, kissed her passionately, and then fled with her treasure.

The day of the ball arrived. Mme. Loisel was a great success. She was prettier than them all, elegant, gracious, smiling, and crazy with joy. All the men looked at her and asked her name, wanting to be introduced. All the attachés of the Cabinet wanted to waltz with her, even the minister himself.

She danced with passion, made drunk by pleasure, forgetting all in the triumph of her beauty, in the glory of her success, in a sort of cloud of happiness composed of all this admiration, of all these awakened desires, and of that sense of complete victory which was so sweet to her heart. This was her ultimate moment.

Comprehension

1. Who is the story about? What kind of woman was she?
2. Why was she so unhappy?
3. What did she think when she thought of her maid?
4. What did she long for?
5. What did her husband bring home to her? What was her reaction?
6. How did her husband try to console her?
7. When she complained that she had no jewels, what did her husband suggest?
8. How did she solve her problem of having no jewelry?
9. Which piece of jewelry did she finally choose?
10. Describe Mme. Loisel's time at the ball.

PART TWO

She left about four o'clock in the morning. Her husband had been sleeping since midnight in a little deserted room with three other gentlemen whose wives were having a very good time. He threw over her shoulders the coat which he had brought. Its poverty contrasted with the elegance of the ball dress. She felt this and wanted to escape so as not to be seen by the other women, who were wrapped in costly furs.

Loisel held her back.

"Wait a bit. You will catch cold outside. I will go and call a cab."

But she did not listen to him and rapidly descended the stairs. When they were in the street they did not find a carriage; and they began to look for one, shouting after the cabmen whom they saw passing by at a distance.

They went down toward the Seine in despair, shivering with cold. At last they found one of those ancient taxis which look as though they can carry only poor people.

It took them to their door in the Rue des Martyrs, and once more, sadly, they climbed up homeward. All was ended for her. And he reflected that he must be at the Ministry at ten o'clock.

She removed the wraps which covered her shoulders before the glass so as once more to see herself in all her glory. But suddenly she uttered a cry. She no longer had the necklace around her neck!

Her husband, already half undressed, demanded, "What is the matter with you?"

She turned madly towards him. "I have—I have—I've lost Mme. Forestier's necklace!"

He stood up, distracted. "What!—How?—Impossible!"

And they looked in the folds of her dress, in the folds of her cloak, in her pockets, everywhere. They did not find it.

He asked, "You're sure you had it on when you left the ball?"

"Yes, I felt it in the vestibule of the palace."

"But if you had lost it in the street, we would have heard it fall. It must be in the cab."

"Yes. Probably. Did you take his number?"

"No. And you, didn't you notice it?"

"No."

They looked at one another, thunderstruck. At last Loisel put on his clothes.

"I will go back on foot," he said, "over the whole route which we have taken to see if I can find it."

And he went out. She sat waiting on a chair in her ball dress, without strength to go to bed, overwhelmed, without fire, without a thought.

Her husband came back about seven o'clock. He had found nothing.

He went to Police Headquarters and to the newspaper offices to offer a reward; he went to the cab companies—everywhere, in fact, where he was urged by the least suspicion of hope.

She waited all day, in the same condition of mad fear before this terrible calamity.

Loisel returned at night with a hollow, pale face; he had discovered nothing.

"You must write to your friend," he said, "that you have broken the clasp of her necklace and that you are having it mended. That will give us time to find it."

She wrote at his dictation.

At the end of a week they had lost all hope. And Loisel, who had aged five years, declared, "We must consider how to replace that ornament."

The next day they took the box which had contained it, and

47

they went to the jeweler whose name was found within. He consulted his books.

"It was not I, madame, who sold that necklace; I must simply have furnished the case."

Then they went from jeweler to jeweler, searching for a necklace like the other, consulting their memories, both of them sick with chagrin and anguish.

In a shop at the Palais Royal, they found a string of diamonds which seemed to them exactly like the one they looked for. It was worth forty thousand francs. They could have it for thirty-six.

So they begged the jeweler not to sell it for three more days. And they made a bargain that he would buy it back for thirty-four thousand francs in case they found the other one before the end of February.

Loisel had eighteen thousand francs which his father had left him. He would borrow the rest.

He did borrow, asking a thousand francs of one person, five hundred of another, five louis here, three louis there. He took up very large loans. He compromised all the rest of his life and, frightened by the pains which were yet to come, by the black misery which he was to suffer, he went to get the new necklace, putting down upon the merchant's counter thirty-six thousand francs.

When Mme. Loisel took back the necklace, Mme. Forestier said to her in a chilly manner, "You should have returned it sooner; I might have needed it."

She did not open the case as her friend had feared. If she had detected the substitution, what would she have thought? What would she have said? Would she have thought that Mme. Loisel was a thief?

Mme. Loisel now knew the horrible existence of the impoverished. She carried her burden, however, with heroism. That dreadful debt had to be paid, and she would pay it. The Loisels fired their servant. They moved from their comfortable apartment to a small attic-like flat under the roof.

She came to know what heavy housework meant and she came to know the hateful chores of the kitchen. She washed the dishes, breaking her beautiful nails on the greasy pots and pans. She washed the dirty linen, the shirts, and the dishcloths, which she dried on a line. She carried the garbage down to the street every morning and carried up the water, stopping at every landing to catch her breath. And, dressed like a poor woman of the streets, she went to the grocer, the butcher, and the fruit vender, carrying her basket on her arm, bargaining, shouting, and defending every sou which she had to spend on food.

Each month they had to pay off some old debts, renew others, and make some new ones.

Her husband worked in the evening as a bookkeeper, and late at night he copied manuscripts for people at five sous a page.

This life lasted for ten years.

At the end of the ten years they had paid everything, the principal on their many loans and the terribly high interest, too.

Mme. Loisel looked old now. She had become the woman of poor households—strong and hard and rough. With frowsy hair, skirts askew, and red hands, she talked loud while washing the floor with great swishes of water. But sometimes, when her husband was at the office, she sat down near the window and thought of that gay evening of long ago, of that ball where she had been so beautiful.

What would have happened if she had not lost that necklace? Who knows? Who knows? How life is strange and changeful! How little a thing is needed for us to be lost or to be saved!

But, one Sunday, having gone to take a walk in the Champs Elysées to refresh herself from the labor of the week, she suddenly saw a woman who was leading a child. It was Mme. Forestier, still young, still beautiful, still charming.

Mme. Loisel felt moved. Was she going to speak to her? Yes, certainly. And now that she had paid, she was going to tell her all about it. Why not?

She went up.

"Good day, Jeanne."

The other, astonished to be familiarly addressed by this plain housewife, did not recognize her at all and stammered, "But—madame!—I do not know—You must be mistaken."

"No. I am Mathilde Loisel."

Her friend uttered a cry.

"Oh, my poor Mathilde! How you are changed!"

"Yes, I have had hard days since I saw you, terrible days—and because of you!"

"Of me! How so?"

"Do you remember that diamond necklace which you lent me to wear at the ministerial ball?"

"Yes. Well?"

"Well, I lost it."

"What do you mean? You brought it back."

"I brought you back another just like it. And for this we have been ten years paying. You can understand that it was not easy for us, us who had nothing. At last it is ended, and I am very glad."

Mme. Forestier had stopped.

"You say that you bought a necklace of diamonds to replace mine?"

"Yes. You never noticed it, then! They were very like."

And she smiled with a joy which was proud and naïve at once.

Mme. Forestier, strongly moved, took her two hands.

"Oh, my poor Mathilde! Why, my necklace was paste. It was worth at most five hundred francs!"

Comprehension and Discussion

1. When did the Loisels leave the ball? Where did Mme. Loisel find her husband at that hour?
2. How did they get home?
3. What did they discover when they arrived home? What was their reaction?
4. What happened at the shop at the Palais Royal?
5. How did Loisel get the money to pay the jeweler?
6. How did they repay their debts? How long did it take?
7. What did Mme. Loisel and Mme. Forestier say to each other when they met after ten years?
8. Many of de Maupassant's stories have "messages." What do you think the message of this story was?
9. Do you know people who think the way Mme. Loisel did at the beginning of the story? What are they like?
10. Have you ever lost or damaged something which you had borrowed from someone else? What did you do about it?

Exercises

A. Use each of the following terms in a sentence:
destiny, distinguished, proper station, elegant, instinct, disdain, impatiently, filled with anguish, colleague, to waltz, at a distance, no longer, cloak, thunderstruck, the whole route, to be worth (a sum of money), before the end of, merchant, suddenly.

B. Circle the term in the right column that has a SIMILAR meaning to the term on the left.

Example: impoverished   ill/(poor)/rich/old

 1. tear   rip/mend/wear/use
 2. askew   neat/happy/messy/new
 3. astonish   bring/shock/hear/recognize
 4. naïve   old/pretty/cynical/unsophisticated
 5. dreadful   expensive/horrible/mysterious/suspicious
 6. annoy   bother/please/worry/humiliate
 7. attaché   servant/taxi driver/diplomat/dancer
 8. sum   household/amount/necklace/linen
 9. colleague   maid/fellow worker/Cabinet official/cabman
 10. precious   silver/inexpensive/ancient/valuable

C. Fill in the blanks with the correct form of the verb in parentheses.

Example: She had him _____(search) the route thoroughly.
   (She had him search the route thoroughly.)

 1. The loss made her _____(feel) very sad.
 2. It wasn't easy, but her husband got her _____ (go) to the ball.
 3. He wants us _____(lend) him the money.
 4. She had a necklace _____(give) to her.
 5. She had her dress _____(deliver) by the store.
 6. They had their house _____(sell) by an agent.
 7. They had their manuscripts _____(copy) by Loisel.
 8. She got her friend _____(loan) her a necklace.
 9. I get my suits _____(clean) by that store.
 10. We make the dog _____(run) in the field for his exercise.

D. Place the adjective in parentheses in its proper position in the sentence.

Example: They live in a big house. (brick)
   (They live in a big brick house.)

 1. I have something to tell you. (pleasant)
 2. She just bought a new dress. (silk)
 3. He prefers to use heavy pots for cooking. (copper)
 4. My sister has a new sports car. (red)

5. There is something happening at the corner. (strange)
6. He knew something was going to happen to him. (bad)
7. Something was blocking their way. (heavy)
8. A merchant sold them the jewels. (agreeable)
9. Do you want to buy a dark coat? (blue)
10. There is no longer a fence around their house. (white)

Unit 7: David Swan

Nathaniel Hawthorne

Nathaniel Hawthorne (1804–1864) wrote many short stories, but he is mostly known for his novels, which include The Scarlet Letter *and* The House of the Seven Gables. *He also served as an American diplomat in London under President Franklin Pierce.*

PART ONE

We know very little about the events which influence our course through life. Some of these events—if such they can be called —come very close to us but pass us by without apparent result and often without any indication of their coming or going. If we knew all the possible changes in our fortune, life would be too full of hopes and fears, of surprises and disappointments, to permit us a single hour of peace. This idea may be illustrated by a page from the history of David Swan.

We have nothing to do with David Swan until we find him at the age of twenty on the main road from his home to the city of Boston where his uncle, a businessman, is going to give him work in the store which he owns. It is enough to say that David was a native of the state of New Hampshire, that he was born of good parents, and that he had received an ordinary school education. After traveling on foot from early morning until noon on a summer day, he felt tired and warm, and he decided to sit down in the first convenient shady place and wait for the coming of the stagecoach in order to ride the remaining distance. Thus he soon came upon a pleasant spot near a spring of water surrounded by a group of shady trees. The place was quiet and cool. He kneeled down at the spring and drank deeply of the fresh water. Then he lay on the soft earth and, resting his head upon a pair of trousers and some shirts which he carried with him in a small package, he fell into a deep sleep.

While he lay asleep in the shade, other people were wide awake and passing along the road, some in one direction, some in the opposite direction; some traveled on foot, others on horseback and in various kinds of vehicles. Some did not look to the right or left; others, when they passed where David was sleeping, glanced in his direction but did not notice him. Some laughed when they saw how deeply he slept. A middle-aged widow, when nobody else was near, stopped and looked at him tenderly and said to herself that the young fellow looked charming in his sleep. A minister, who was very much opposed to strong drink, saw him and thought he was drunk. The next Sunday he mentioned poor David in his church sermon as an awful example of the results of strong drink.

David had slept only a short time when a rich-looking carriage, drawn by two fine horses, stopped directly in front of where he slept. One of the horses had injured his leg and the driver wished to let the horse rest for a while. An elderly businessman and his wife got out of the carriage and decided to rest during this time under the shade of the trees. There they noticed the spring and David asleep alongside of it. They tried to walk lightly and to make as little noise as possible in order not to wake him.

"How deeply he sleeps," said the old gentleman. "How quietly and easily he breathes. If I could sleep as deeply as that, I would be very happy, for such sleep, without the help of sleeping medicines, indicates good health and a mind without troubles."

"And youth besides," said his wife. "Old people like us never sleep like that."

The old couple became more and more interested in the unknown youth who lay there sleeping so peacefully.

"It seems to me," said the woman at last to her husband, "that he strongly resembles our own dear son. Shall we wake him up?"

"For what purpose?" said the husband. "We know nothing of his character."

"That honest face," answered his wife in a quiet voice. "This innocent sleep!"

While the conversation was going on, David did not move, nor did the features of his face indicate that he knew that two people were looking at him with great interest. Nevertheless, Fortune was standing very close to him, for the old man and his wife were very rich. Their only son had recently died, and there was no one in their family to whom they wanted to leave all their money. In such cases, people sometimes do stranger things than to wake up a young man, accept him as their own son, and later make him the heir to all their riches.

"Shall we wake him up?" repeated the lady.

But suddenly the driver of the coach said, "We are ready now, sir. The horse is rested."

The old couple stopped speaking suddenly, looked at each other with some surprise, and then hurried toward the coach. Once inside the coach, the whole idea of making David their son now seemed to them quite ridiculous, and they were surprised that such a strange thought could have come to their minds. Soon the man began to tell his wife about a plan he had to leave all his money, when he died, for the establishment of a large charitable institution. Meanwhile, David went on enjoying his quiet sleep.

Comprehension

1. Do you agree with the thoughts in the first paragraph? What do you think about this?
2. Who was David Swan? What do we know about him?
3. When he got tired, what did he do?
4. What did the minister do when he saw David asleep?
5. Why did the carriage stop near David?

6. Who got out of the carriage? What did they do?
7. What was David doing while the couple were talking about him?
8. Why were they interested in David?
9. Why did they leave when they did? What had they decided?
10. What did the couple decide to do instead?

PART TWO

Not more than five minutes passed when a young girl came along. She had a light and easy step which showed at once the happiness of her spirit. She was very pretty. She stopped to drink at the spring and was naturally surprised to find David sleeping there. At first she felt as if she had entered, without permission, into a gentleman's bedroom, and she was about to leave quietly when she saw an enormous bee buzzing around the head of the sleeper. Quickly but quietly, she attacked the bee with her handkerchief and drove him away. How sweet a picture! This good act completed, the girl looked tenderly for a moment at David.

"He is handsome," she said to herself.

But David did not move, nor did he smile. No look of appreciation or of welcome appeared upon his face. Perhaps the girl was the girl of his dreams, the girl with whom he might spend a life of happiness, if only he could awake and speak to her.

"How deeply he sleeps," said the girl.

She left, but she appeared thoughtful, and now she did not seem as light or happy as she had a few moments ago.

She walked slowly back to the nearby village where she had a thriving dry goods store. It's too bad, she thought. He might be just the sort of young man I'm looking for to help out in the store. I wonder if I would have fallen in love with him and married him, she silently thought, a dreamy look in her eye.

The girl was hardly out of sight when two men turned from the road to stop a moment in the shade. Both had dark faces, and both wore caps which they pulled down well over their eyes. They wore old clothes. These men were robbers who were ready to steal anything they found and to kill anyone who might try to stop them. Seeing David asleep alongside the spring, one of them said to his companion, "Look, do you see that package under his head?"

"Yes, perhaps he has a wallet or some money hidden inside of it," said the other. "Or perhaps he has some money in one of his pockets."

"But what if he wakes up?" said the first.

His companion pulled out a long knife from his belt and pointed it at David.

"This will take care of him," he said.

They approached the sleeping David and prepared to remove the package from under his head. David continued to sleep tranquilly.

"You take the package. If he moves, I'll strike," said the man with the knife.

But, at this moment, a dog ran in from the road to drink at the spring. The dog paid no attention to the men nor to David but drank thirstily of the water. The men stopped suddenly and one of them drew a pistol from his pocket.

"Wait!" said the other man. "We can do nothing now. The owner of the dog is probably close behind."

"Yes," said the other. "We'd better get out of here."

Thus the two men left as stealthily as they had come and continued down the road. In a few minutes, they had forgotten the entire event—and, of course, there was one less dark crime to be written against their names in the books of heaven, but of this they did not think for even a moment.

David slept, but no longer as quietly as at first. He had had an hour's peaceful sleep and was now more rested. He moved slightly and lay for a few minutes half asleep, half awake. Then suddenly in the distance there was a loud noise of approaching wheels. The stagecoach was coming. David jumped up and ran out just in time to call to the driver.

"Hello, driver! Have you room for one more passenger?"

"There is room on top," answered the driver.

David climbed to the top of the coach and the driver started off. The coach moved quickly down the road, and David did not give even a final glance to the place where he had slept. He was thinking now of other things, of the life ahead of him. He had no memories of the place where he had rested because he had no knowledge of anything that had happened there. He did not know that Fortune had smiled on him and almost brought him great riches and a great love with perhaps a successful career in business. He did not know that he had been close to death at the point of a robber's knife—all within the space of one brief hour.

Thus it is that life deals with us in many strange ways. Fortunately, we do not know the many things that come close to us and pass us by without results. If we knew all the many possibilities of change in our fortune, life would be too full of hopes and fears, surprises and disappointments to permit us a single hour of peace.

Comprehension and Discussion

1. What was the girl like who came along?
2. What did she do when she saw the bee?
3. What thoughts did the girl have as she left?
4. Who were the two men who came next? What did they look like?
5. What were they going to do to David?
6. How was he saved?
7. What happened when David woke up?
8. What do you think the author was trying to tell us in this story?
9. What are some things that might have happened to you if you had been aware of them?
10. Tell of a time when you fell asleep in an unusual place.

Exercises

A. Use each of the following terms in a sentence:
to pass us by, coming or going, on foot, convenient, spring of water, middle-aged, strong drink, carriage, innocent, Fortune, ridiculous, buzzing, appreciation, thriving, to fall in love, tranquilly, thirstily, had better do something, just in time.

B. Give two negative forms for each of the following sentences.

Example: I see someone over there.
(I don't see anyone over there.)
(I see no one over there.)

1. There is someone at the door.
2. There was somebody sleeping by the side of the road.
3. She has some money in the bank.
4. I have somebody in mind for that job.
5. We saw some stores.
6. We can do something about it.
7. I have something to do now.
8. There is some bread in the refrigerator; there's some on the table, too.

9. He has something to give you.
10. They have gone somewhere.

C. Circle the word on the right that RHYMES with the word on the left.

Example: I'd   led/lad/(lied)/lid

1. I'll   hill/mail/mile/feel
2. laugh   ought/rough/half/saw
3. owe   sew/new/two/saw
4. kneeled   killed/needed/solid/field
5. heir   ear/there/or/are
6. buzz   buys/does/goes/sneeze
7. does   is/goes/laws/was
8. we'd   led/word/wide/need
9. I'm   him/time/came/jam
10. you're   our/year/door/fire

D. Circle the term on the right that has the SAME meaning as the word on the left.

Example: cancel   put away/look up/look over/(call off)

1. promise   give one's word/hesitate/refuse/deny
2. fortunate   early/lucky/late/famous
3. occurred   arrived/delayed/happened/walked
4. at once   one time later/seldom/immediately/later
5. elderly   young/middle-aged/old/charming
6. event   change/occurrence/accident/surprise
7. evidently   always/probably/seldom/apparently
8. grateful   thankful/agreeable/hopeful/disappointed
9. confused   mixed up/worn out/uneasy/difficult
10. main   fresh/remaining/native/principal

Unit 8: Rip Van Winkle

Washington Irving

In his character of Rip, Washington Irving (1783–1859) created an interesting man who has been known to schoolchildren for more than 160 years.

PART ONE

Rip Van Winkle was a gentle, good-natured man who was a kind neighbor and an obedient husband. He was a poor man, but most people loved him, and he was a favorite among children.

One fine autumn day, Rip climbed to one of the highest parts of the Catskill Mountains. He was doing what he liked to do— hunting squirrels—and the quiet woods echoed and re-echoed with the sound of his gun. Out of breath and tired, he lay down on the green grass at the top of the hill. From here he looked out over all the lower country for many miles. He saw the noble Hudson River far, far below him, moving slowly along. He looked down the other side into a deep valley. The bottom of the valley was filled with rocks which had fallen from the mountains above. For some time, Rip lay there half asleep. Evening was approaching, and the mountains began to throw their long, blue shadows over the valley. Rip saw that it would be dark long before he reached the valley, and he sighed deeply when he thought about Mrs. Van Winkle.

He started to go down the valley when he heard a voice calling, "Rip Van Winkle! Rip Van Winkle!" He looked around but could see nothing except a lone bird flying across the mountains. He thought that he had been mistaken and began again to descend when he heard the same voice: "Rip Van Winkle! Rip Van Winkle!" At the same time, his dog Wolf gave a low bark and came close to his side. Rip now began to feel a little afraid. He looked anxiously into the valley and then saw a strange little man slowly climbing up the mountainside and carrying something heavy on his back. Rip was surprised to see anyone in this lonely place, but he thought it was possibly one of his neighbors in need of some help, so he hurried down to meet him.

As he came nearer, he was greatly surprised at the strangeness of the man's appearance. The man was a short, square-built old fellow with thick hair and a beard. He was dressed in the old Dutch fashion. He wore a very short coat and several pairs of trousers. The outer trousers were very large and were decorated with rows of buttons down the sides. This strange little man carried on his back a small barrel that seemed full of liquor, and he motioned for Rip to come and help him. Rip was rather afraid, but as usual he was always ready to assist anyone. He helped the man, and together they proceeded up the mountain. They proceeded some distance along what seemed to be the dry bed of a former mountain stream. Occasionally Rip heard what sounded like distant thunder, although the skies were clear and there were no signs of storms. These sounds seemed to come from the direction in which they were walking. They passed around the side of the mountain and thus came at last to a level place that resembled a small amphitheater, surrounded by tall trees. All this time Rip and his companion had climbed the mountain in silence. Rip wondered why this stranger was carrying a small barrel of liquor up this wild mountain, but there was something so strange about the unknown man that Rip was deeply impressed and was afraid to speak to him.

When they entered the amphitheater, Rip saw other strange things. In the center was a group of unusual-looking men playing an old Dutch game called ninepins, in which they rolled large balls at small sticks placed upon the ground. All the men were dressed in very strange costumes, similar to the costume of Rip's companion. Their faces, too, were not quite normal. One had a large beard, a broad face, and small eyes like those of a pig. The face of another was almost entirely nose, and he wore a round white hat with a red feather in it. They all had beards of various shapes and colors. There was one who seemed to be the commander. He was a fat old gentleman with a weather-beaten face. He wore a short coat, broad belt, high hat with a feather in it, red stockings, and high-heeled shoes. These men made Rip think of the men in a very old Dutch painting, brought from Holland, that he had once seen.

Rip thought that it was very strange that while these men were amusing themselves, they all had such serious faces and remained so mysteriously silent. Nothing interrupted the quiet except the noise of the balls which echoed along the mountains like thunder and which was the noise which Rip had heard as they came up the mountain.

When Rip and his companion came near, the men stopped playing and stood looking at Rip. They looked at him in such a strange manner and with such strange, deathly faces that Rip's heart turned within him and his knees began to knock together. His companion now emptied the liquor into large bottles and made signs to Rip to wait a moment. Rip obeyed with fear. The strange men drank the liquor in deep silence, and then they returned to their game.

Little by little Rip's fears grew less. He even dared, when no one was looking, to taste the liquor, which was excellent Holland gin. Rip was naturally a thirsty soul, and he soon took another drink. One taste made him want another. He repeated his drinks so often that his eyes swam in his head, his head became heavy, and he fell into a deep sleep.

When he woke up, he found himself back on the green grass from where he had first seen the old man coming towards him up the mountain. He rubbed his eyes. It was a bright, sunny morning. The birds were singing in the trees. "Surely," thought

Rip, "I have not slept here all night." He thought of what had happened before he fell asleep. He remembered the strange man with the small barrel of liquor on his back. He remembered the sad group of men playing ninepins. "Oh, that liquor! That terrible liquor," thought Rip. "What excuse shall I make to my wife?"

He looked around for his gun, but he found only an old rusty one lying beside him. He thought that the strange men whom he had met had played a trick on him. They had given him liquor and then stolen his gun. Wolf, too, had disappeared, but he possibly had gone after a squirrel. Rip whistled for his dog and shouted his name. The echoes repeated his whistle and shout, but no dog came.

He decided to go where he had been last evening, and if he found any of the men, he would demand his dog and gun. As he got up to walk, however, he found that his legs and his whole body were stiff.

"These mountain beds do not agree with me," thought Rip. With great difficulty, he climbed the mountain along the route that he and his companion had taken the night before. To his great surprise, he found a stream of water now running where last night there had only been the dry bed. He finally came to the amphitheater, but it was now filled with trees and great stones. He again called and whistled for his dog, but there was no answer. It was now almost noon and Rip was very hungry. He did not wish to lose his dog and gun and he was afraid to meet his wife, but he also did not want to die of hunger. He shook his head, put his rusty gun on his shoulder, and, with a heart full of trouble, started down the mountain.

As Rip approached the village, he met a number of people whom he did not know. This surprised him, for he thought he knew everyone in the surrounding country. The people's clothes were different from those to which he was accustomed. They all looked at him in a very strange way. They did this so often that finally Rip passed his hand over his face to find out what was wrong and discovered, to his surprise, that his beard had grown a foot long.

Comprehension

1. What kind of a man was Rip Van Winkle? Did people like him?
2. Where did Rip go hunting? What did he hunt for?

3. What happened when he started to go down the mountain?
4. What was odd about the little man's appearance?
5. Where did they walk to?
6. What did Rip see when they arrived?
7. How did he act with the unusual little people?
8. How did Rip fall asleep?
9. What did he say when he awakened?
10. What happened when Rip had descended the mountain? How had he and the people changed?

PART TWO

Rip now came to the edge of the village. A crowd of strange children ran after him, shouting and pointing at his gray beard. The dogs, too, which he did not recognize, barked at him as he passed. The village itself was changed; it was larger and there were more people. There were houses which he had never seen before, and the houses which he had known so well had disappeared. Rip couldn't believe his eyes. Surely this was his native village, which he had left only the day before! There stood the Catskill Mountains—there was the beautiful Hudson River. Rip was badly confused. "That bottle of liquor last night," he thought, "has mixed up my poor head badly."

At last, with great difficulty, Rip found the way to his own house, expecting every minute to hear the sharp voice of Mrs. Van Winkle. He found the house, but the roof had fallen in and the windows and doors were broken. The house was also empty and abandoned. He went in and called loudly for his wife and children; the lonely rooms rang for a moment with his voice, and then all was silence.

Next, he hurried toward the old village inn—but that was gone. In its place was a large building with big windows and over the door a sign reading The Union Hotel. Instead of the great tree under which Rip and his friends used to sit and smoke, there was now a tall pole with a strange-looking flag of stars and stripes. There was also a crowd of people around the door, but Rip did not recognize any of them. The very character of the people seemed to have changed. They were all busy and hurrying about instead of quietly sitting and smoking long Dutch pipes. He looked for Nicholas Vedder and for Von Bummel, the schoolmaster, but they were not there.

Rip Van Winkle, with his long beard, his rusty gun, his old clothes, and so many children at his heels, soon attracted the attention of the people at the door of the inn. They crowded around him and looked at him from head to foot with great curiosity. They began to ask questions about politics, and one man asked him on which side he was going to vote in the elections. Rip could not understand these questions.

"But what has brought you to the election with a gun on your shoulder and a crowd of people at your heels?" asked a second man in a severe tone.

"I am a poor, quiet man—and a native of this place," explained Rip.

"But where did you come from and what do you want?"

Rip assured them that he was simply looking for some of his neighbors who always used to sit on the bench in front of the inn.

Someone said, "Well, who are they? Name them."

Rip thought a moment and asked, "Where's Nicholas Vedder?"

There was a silence in the crowd and no one seemed to recognize the name. Then an old man replied in a thin voice, "Nicholas Vedder? Oh, he has been dead and buried some eighteen years."

"Where's Brom Dutcher?" asked Rip.

"Oh, he went off to the army at the beginning of the war. Some say he was killed, others say he was drowned—but he never came back again."

"Where's Von Bummel, the schoolmaster?"

"He went off to the war, too, was a great general, and he is now in Congress."

Rip's heart died within him when he heard of these sad changes in his home and friends. He was alone in the world. Also, he was confused by the fact that Nicholas Vedder had been dead for eighteen years. And what army and what war were they talking about? What did they mean by "Congress"? But Rip had no courage to ask for any more friends, and he cried out at last in despair.

"But does nobody here know Rip Van Winkle?"

"Oh, Rip Van Winkle," said two or three. "That's Rip Van Winkle over there, standing against that tree."

Rip looked and saw an exact image of himself as he was when he went up the mountain, apparently as lazy and certainly as poorly dressed. Poor Rip was now completely confused. He doubted his own identity. Was he himself or was he another man? Suddenly someone asked him who he really was and what his name was.

"God knows," replied Rip. "I'm not myself. I'm somebody else. That's me over there. No, it's somebody else in my shoes. I was myself last night, but I fell asleep on the mountain, and they have changed my gun and taken my dog. Everything is changed, and I'm changed, and I can't tell who I really am."

The people began to exchange glances with one another as if to say that they thought the poor old fellow was crazy. At this moment, a good-looking young woman pushed her way through the crowd in order to get a look at the old man. She had a child in her arms who became frightened when he saw Rip and began to cry. "Quiet, Rip," the young woman said to the child. "Don't cry. The old man won't hurt you." The name of the child, the manner of the mother, and the tone of her voice awakened memories in Rip's mind.

"What is your name, my good woman?" he asked.

"Judith Gardinier."

"And what was your father's name?"

"Oh, poor man, his name was Rip Van Winkle, but he went away from home twenty years ago with his gun, and no one has seen him since. His dog came home without him, but I don't know whether he shot himself or was captured by the Indians. Nobody knows. I was only a girl when he went away."

Rip had only one more question to ask, and he asked it with a trembling voice.

"Where's your mother?"

"Oh," said the young woman, "my mother died a short time ago."

The old man could control himself no longer. He caught his daughter and her child in his arms. "I am your father!" he cried, "I was young Rip Van Winkle once—I am old Rip Van Winkle now. Does nobody here know poor Rip Van Winkle?"

All stood surprised until an old woman, coming out of the crowd, put her hand to her forehead, and looking closely into his face for a moment, said, "Yes, it is Rip Van Winkle. Welcome home again, old neighbor. Where have you been these twenty years?"

Rip soon told his story, for the twenty years seemed to him to be only one night.

To make a long story short, Rip's daughter finally took him home with her and there he continued to live for some years. She had a comfortable little home and a pleasant husband. Rip remembered the husband as one of the small boys who used to climb upon his back.

Rip soon took up his old walks and old habits. He found a few of his old friends, but they were all very old now. Once more he sat on the bench at the inn, but it was a long time before he could understand the strange events that had taken place during his long sleep. There had been a Revolutionary War with England, and now he was a free citizen, of the United States.

Rip used to tell his story to every stranger that arrived at the hotel. At first, he used to vary on some points, but finally it became the exact story which has been told here. Every man, woman, and child in the neighborhood knew it by heart. Some people doubted the truth of the story, but all the old Dutch inhabitants believed it entirely. Even to this day, when they hear a thunderstorm in the Catskills, they say that the strange little men are playing a game of ninepins.

Comprehension and Discussion

1. What seemed new to Rip about his native village?
2. What did he find when he went to his own house?
3. What had changed about the inn? About the people?
4. When Rip asked about three old friends, what did the people tell him?
5. Who was standing against the tree, and why did people point to him?
6. Why did people begin to think Rip was crazy?
7. Who was Judith Gardinier? What did she tell Rip about his wife?
8. What did people believe about Rip's story?
9. Do you think someone could sleep for twenty years? What's the longest you've ever slept?
10. What would it be like for you if you returned to your home twenty years later, as Rip had? What changes do you think you would find?

Exercises

A. Use each of the following terms in a sentence:
squirrel, to approach, beard, to be mistaken, to be dressed in, trousers, ninepins, weather-beaten, high-heeled shoes,

rusty, to bark at, to whistle, to believe one's eyes, to crowd around, at one's heels, as if, thunderstorm.

B. Circle the word on the right that RHYMES with the word on the left.

Example: wrong ping/**long**/hang/rung

1. great   heat/set/hate/height
2. hurried   married/feared/cared/worried
3. beard   feared/bored/cared/bird
4. drowned   grown/loaned/ruined/found
5. knows   news/sews/knees/lose
6. he'll   well/bill/feel/fall
7. war   roar/ware/car/hire
8. thought   though/rough/cough/bought
9. noise   nose/boys/choice/nice
10. sin   rein/keen/bin/mine

C. Make questions from the following sentences. Use a question word to replace the italicized word or phrase.

Example: He went into the forest *many weeks ago.*
        (When did he go into the forest?)

1. He went into the forest *on foot.*
2. They were having a celebration *at the village inn.*
3. He heard *the sound of distant thunder.*
4. Their little village was *in the mountains.*
5. He saw *his wife.*
6. Many strangers stayed *at the hotel.*
7. He liked to walk around the house *at night.*
8. He is going to travel *by ship.*
9. He saw *a flash of lightning.*
10. *An old man* approached the people in front of the hotel.

D. Match the term in the left column with its OPPOSITE in the right column.

Example: _e_ **6.** empty   e. full

___ 1. in front of   a. after
___ 2. thin   b. answer
___ 3. quiet   c. behind
___ 4. find   d. few
___ 5. before   e. full

___ 6. empty   **f.** lose
___ 7. question   **g.** noisy
___ 8. deep   **h.** seldom
___ 9. several   **i.** shallow
___ 10. often   **j.** thick

Unit 9: Two Short Stories by Kate Chopin

Kate Chopin (1851–1904) began writing on the advice of her doctor, who was worried that she was too depressed over the death of her husband. Her feminist themes outraged some readers but brought her critical acclaim.

A Pair of Silk Stockings

Little Mrs. Sommers one day found herself unexpectedly in possession of an extra fifteen dollars. This was an unusually large amount for her, and she felt important as she touched the bulge in her worn old wallet. She had not felt this way in years.

She walked around in a daze, wondering how she should invest this sum. She didn't want to do anything which she would later regret. Indeed, she lay awake for several hours, tossing in her bed, speculating on a proper use for her money.

A dollar or two should be added to the price she usually paid for Janie's shoes so that they would last longer than the cheaper kind. She should also buy some cotton material in order to make new shirts for the boys and for Janie and Mag. She was going to patch their old shirts and make them do, but now, perhaps . . .

Mag should have another nightgown. She had seen some wonderful patterns in a shop window—a real bargain. The girls also needed some new stockings—that would save her some darning for a while. The boys needed new caps. Oh, the vision of her children looking fresh and dainty for once in their lives excited her and kept her awake with anticipation.

The neighbors often spoke of better times for the little woman, times which she had known before she became Mrs. Sommers. She, however, never indulged in that kind of thinking; she had no time to devote to the past. Her vision of the future often seemed like some dim, gaunt monster, and it scared her, but somehow tomorrow never came.

Mrs. Sommers was a person who knew the value of a good bargain, and she knew how to find one. She would stand for hours making her way inch by inch toward some desired object that was selling below cost. She could elbow her way if need be; she had learned to clutch a piece of merchandise and hold it and stick to it with persistence and determination till her turn came to be served, no matter when it came.

But that day she was a little faint and tired. She had swallowed a light lunch—no! When she came to think of it, between getting the children fed and the place righted and preparing herself for the shopping bout, she had actually forgotten to eat any lunch at all!

She sat herself upon a revolving stool before a counter that was comparatively deserted, trying to gather strength and courage to do battle with all the other shoppers who were pushing and shoving to get to the same items she wanted. All of a sudden, she felt weak and limp as she rested her hand aimlessly on the counter. She wore no gloves. Slowly, by degrees, she became aware of what her hand was resting on. It was very soothing and pleasant to touch. She looked down to see that her hand lay on a pile of silk stockings. A sign nearby announced that they had been reduced from $2.50 to $1.98. A young girl behind the counter asked her if she wished to examine their entire selection of silk hosiery. She smiled as though she had just been asked if she wanted to examine a diamond tiara with the intention of buying it. How absurd! But she continued to feel the soft, sheeny, luxurious things—with both hands now, holding them up to see them glisten and to let them glide like small snakes through her fingers.

She blushed as she looked up at the salesperson and asked if they had any in her size, 8½.

In fact, there were more of that size than any other. She looked over the selection of colors carefully, finally holding up a black pair and pretending to examine the texture. The clerk assured her that they were of excellent quality.

Her next few moments happened as though she were dreaming, not in control of her movements or directions. She purchased the black stockings and went immediately to the ladies' room to put them on. She was not thinking at all. She seemed, for a while, to have taken a rest from that tiring activity and to have abandoned herself to some mechanical function which freed her from responsibility.

The stockings felt so good on her flesh! She rose and went directly to the shoe department where she informed the clerk that she wanted a perfect fit and did not mind paying extra as long as she found some good-quality boots.

It was a long time since Mrs. Sommers had been fitted with gloves. On the rare occasions when she had bought a pair, they were always "bargains," so cheap that it would have been preposterous and unreasonable to have expected them to be fitted to the hand.

Now she rested her elbow on the cushion of the glove counter, and a pretty, pleasant young creature, delicate and deft of touch, drew a long-wristed "kid" over Mrs. Sommers' hand. She smoothed it down over the wrist and buttoned it neatly, and both lost themselves for a second or two in admiring contemplation of the little symmetrical gloved hand. But there were other places where money might be spent.

There were books and magazines piled up in the window of a stall a few paces down the street. Mrs. Sommers bought two high-priced magazines such as she had been accustomed to reading in the days when she had been accustomed to other pleasant things. She carried them without wrappings. As well as she could, she lifted her skirts at the crossings. Her stockings and boots and well-fitted gloves had worked marvels in her bearing —had given her a feeling of assurance, a sense of belonging to the well-dressed multitude.

She was very hungry. Another time she would have stilled the cravings for food until reaching her own home, where she would have brewed herself a cup of tea and taken a snack of anything that was available. But the impulses that were guiding her would not allow that today. Today she would go where there was spotless china and shining crystal, where there were soft-stepping waiters and people of fashion.

She went to a restaurant which she often passed but never entered. At first she feared that her entrance would cause a stir. It didn't. She seated herself at a small table alone and was immediately attended by a waiter. She chose a light lunch—nothing which would draw undue attention—and settled back, leisurely removing her gloves and laying them on the table. She slowly paged through her magazine, examined the beautiful plates and glasses, and realized that the restaurant was even more elegant than she had thought from the outside.

She delicately tasted her salad, read her magazine, looked at the fine ladies and gentlemen at the other small tables, sipped her wine, and wiggled her toes in the silk stockings. When the waiter brought the bill, she tipped him generously, and he bowed before her as though she were a princess of royal blood.

She left the restaurant to the pleasing strains of a piano and the soft breezes of the wind outside. Her next temptation came in the form of a marquee.

The play had begun when she entered the theater, and the house seemed to be full. There were, however, a few vacant seats left, and presently she was seated between two women who had gone to the play only because they had nothing better to do. The people around her seemed to be there only to display their gaudy dress or to eat candy. Certainly no one there absorbed the surroundings in quite the same way as Mrs. Sommers. She gathered in the players and the stage in one wide impression and seemed to swallow it all. She laughed and wept and even enjoyed talking to some gaudy women afterwards about the better parts of the play.

When the show ended and everyone filed out of the theater, it was like a dream ended. People scattered in all directions, and Mrs. Sommers went to the corner to wait for the cable car.

A man with keen eyes sat across from her and stared. He seemed both interested and delighted by the look in her eyes. But he was also puzzled by what he saw there . . . or thought he saw. What was there was a poignant wish, a powerful longing that the cable car would never stop anywhere, but go on with her forever.

Comprehension

1. Why was Mrs. Sommers walking around in a daze?
2. Where did she think she should spend her money?
3. How many children did Mrs. Sommers have? What were the names of the girls?
4. What was Mrs. Sommers' attitude toward her past? Her future?
5. How good a shopper was Mrs. Sommers? How did she find bargains?
6. What did she buy first? How much were they marked down?
7. What did she buy next? How did these things make her feel?
8. What kind of restaurant did she go to?
9. Describe her behavior at the table while eating.
10. Why did Mrs. Sommers long for an endless cable car ride?

Madame Célestin's Divorce

Madame Célestin always wore a neat and snug-fitting robe when she went out in the morning to sweep her small gallery. Lawyer Paxton liked her best in the blue one with pink ribbons at the neck. He thought she looked graceful and beautiful. She was always sweeping her gallery when Lawyer Paxton passed by in the morning on his way to his office at St. Denis Street.

Sometimes he stopped and leaned over the fence to say good morning at his ease; to criticize or admire her rosebushes; or, when he had enough time, to hear what she had to say. Madame Célestin usually had a good deal to say. She would gather up the train of her blue robe in one hand and, balancing the broom gracefully on the other, would go tripping down to where the lawyer leaned, as comfortably as he could, over her picket fence.

Of course she had talked to him of her troubles. Everyone knew of Madame Célestin's troubles.

"Really, madame," he told her once, in his deliberate, calculating lawyer-tone, "it's more than human nature—woman's nature—should be called upon to endure. Here you are, working your fingers off"—she glanced down at two rosy fingertips that showed through the rents of her baggy doeskin gloves—"taking in sewing, giving music lessons, doing God knows what in the way of manual labor to support yourself and those two little ones." Madame Célestin's pretty face beamed with satisfaction at this enumeration of her trials.

"You are right, Judge. Nothing. Not one penny have I seen in these past four months from the man I call my husband. He hasn't sent me a single thing."

"The scoundrel," muttered Lawyer Paxton.

"And what's more," she continued, "people say he's making money down in Alexandria. Plenty of it. When he wants to work, that is."

"You probably haven't seen him for about six months," suggested the lawyer. Madame Célestin nodded in agreement as he continued. "That's it. That's what I've been telling you these past few weeks. He has practically deserted you. He fails to support you. It wouldn't surprise me to learn that he has mistreated you."

"Well, you know, Judge," she said with an evasive cough, "a man that drinks—what can you expect? And if you only knew the promises that he's made to me! Ah, if I had a dollar for every one of those promises, I'd be a rich woman and wouldn't have to do all this work!"

"In my opinion, madame, you would be foolish to endure it any longer, especially when you have the alternative of divorce. It's there so that people like you can be helped."

"You spoke about that before, Judge, and now I think you may be right." Madame Célestin talked more about divorce with Lawyer Paxton, and they both got very interested in the possibility.

"You know, about that divorce," Madame Célestin said the next morning, "I've been talking to my family and my friends about it, and they're all against it."

"That's to be expected, madame, in this community of Creoles. I know you'll face opposition; you'll have to be brave and face it."

"Oh, don't worry, I'm going to face it. Grandmother says it would be a disgrace, that no one in our family has ever been divorced. That's easy for her to say. What trouble has she ever had? She also says that I must go consult with Father Ducheron;

he's my confessor, you understand. Well, I'll go, Judge, to please Grandmother, but all the confessors in the world aren't going to make me change my mind. I'm not going to put up with that man any longer."

A day or two later, she was waiting for him again. "You know, Judge, about that divorce."

"Yes, yes," responded the lawyer. He was pleased to see determination in her brown eyes and in the curves of her pretty mouth. "I suppose you had to see Father Ducheron and be brave?"

"Oh, he gave me a sermon that I thought would never end. He spoke of scandal and setting a bad example. Finally, he washed his hands of the problem, telling me that he was through with me and that I would have to see the bishop."

"You won't let the bishop talk you out of it, will you?" stammered the lawyer, more nervously than he could understand.

"You don't know me yet, Judge," laughed Madame Célestin with a turn of her head and a wave of her broom as she walked back into the house.

"Well, Madame Célestin! What happened with the bishop?" He was standing there anxiously. She had not seen him, but when she did, she immediately rushed to him. His heart fluttered.

"Yes, I saw him," she began. The lawyer had already decided that she was still determined by the look on her face. "Ah, he's an eloquent man. Probably the most eloquent man in the whole county. I cried when I told him of my troubles, and he was very understanding. I think he feels for me. Then he spoke of the danger of the move I want to make. Of the temptation, too. It would have moved you, Judge. He told me that it was the duty of Catholics to put up with trials and pain and that I would have to lead a life of self-denial. He told me all that."

"But he hasn't shaken your resolve, I see," the lawyer said with a smile.

"That's for sure," she returned emphatically. "That bishop doesn't know what it's like to be married to a man like my husband and to have to endure my sorrow. The Pope himself can't make me put up with that any longer if you say that I have a legal right to end this marriage."

A noticeable change had come over Lawyer Paxton. He discarded his workday coat and began to wear his Sunday one to the office. He grew solicitous as to the shine of his boots, his collar, and the set of his tie. He brushed and trimmed his whiskers with a care that had not before been apparent. Then he fell into a stupid habit of dreaming as he walked the streets of the old town. It would be good to take unto himself a wife, he dreamed. And he could dream of no other than pretty Madame Célestin filling that sweet and sacred office as she filled his thoughts now. Old Natchitoches would not hold them comfortably, perhaps; but the world was surely wide enough to live in, outside of Natchitoches town.

His heart beat in a strangely irregular manner as he neared Madame Célestin's house one morning and discovered her behind the rosebushes, as usual plying her broom. She had finished the gallery and steps and was sweeping the little brick walk along the edge of the violet border.

"Good morning, Madame Célestin."

"Ah, it's you, Judge. Good morning." He waited. She seemed to be doing the same. Then she ventured, with some hesitancy. "You know, Judge, about that divorce. I've been thinking. Maybe you'd better forget about it." She was making deep rings in the palm of her hand with the end of the broom and examining them critically. Her face seemed to be particularly rosy this morning. "Yes, I suppose you'd better just forget all about that divorce talk. You see, Judge, my husband came home last night."

"But what difference does that make?" The lawyer practically shouted the question.

"He's promised me on his word of honor that he's going to turn over a new leaf."

Comprehension and Discussion

1. When did Madame Célestin and Lawyer Paxton see each other? What was she usually doing?
2. What was her relationship with her husband like?
3. Why did the lawyer urge her to consider divorce?
4. What did her family and friends say about her plan? What did her grandmother say?
5. What did the two priests tell her about her plan?
6. What was the lawyer hoping would happen? Why?
7. How do you feel about divorce? How does your family feel?
8. How were the two women in these stories alike? How were they different?
9. We know that the first story is almost one hundred years

77

old. If you were rewriting it today, what figure would you use instead of fifteen dollars?

10. Why do you think these kinds of short stories disturbed the author's contemporaries?

Exercises

A. Use each of the following terms in a sentence:
feminist, bulge, to walk around in a daze, to speculate, to last longer, to make something do, dainty, limp, aimlessly, hosiery, to glisten, in fact, as though, on rare occasions, china, crystal, fashion, scoundrel, what's more, evasive, resolve, to turn over a new leaf.

B. Fill in the blanks in the table with the appropriate form of the word.

	Noun	Adjective	Adverb
Example:	curiosity	curious	curiously
1.		enthusiastic	
2.			nervously
3.	evasiveness		
4.	anxiety		
5.	criticism		
6.		comfortable	
7.		stupid	
8.			sorrowfully
9.			eternally
10.	absence		

C. Change the following sentences from the active to the passive voice.

Example: Madame picked up the broom.
(The broom was picked up by Madame.)

1. She sweeps her gallery every day.
2. The bishop gave her a sermon.
3. He shined his boots.
4. She bought a pair of soft gloves.
5. She will buy a new nightgown.
6. The usher seated her between two other women.
7. Did she wear a blue robe?
8. The future did not scare her.
9. He has practically deserted you.
10. He walks the dog in the morning.

78

D. Change the following statements to questions.

Example: She is sweeping her gallery.
(Is she sweeping her gallery?)

1. The play had already begun when she entered.
2. She has spoken to a priest about her divorce.
3. He promises to turn over a new leaf.
4. The stockings felt good on her skin.
5. I should take the case to the court.
6. She was deserted by her husband.
7. The patrons are dressed in gaudy clothes.
8. You aren't happy with the results.
9. There weren't any friends who agreed with her.
10. She hasn't been happy these past six months.

Unit 10: The Lady or the Tiger

Frank R. Stockton

Frank R. Stockton (1834–1902) wrote many fanciful, humorous, and fantastic stories, but this is his only famous one. When it was published, readers immediately decided that it had deep moral and psychological implications.

PART ONE

Long, long ago there lived a king who was crude and very much like a savage. He had learned some manners from his Latin neighbors, but mostly he was barbaric, loud, and gruff. He had none of the grace and polish of his neighbors. He was a man of great fancies and even greater enthusiasm. Because he had so much authority as a king, he was able to force some of these fancies into reality. Or at least he tried to.

His personality was normally calm when everything was in order. When there was a little hitch, however, he was exultant and happy. He loved it when things went wrong because that meant that he could then correct them. He loved to make the crooked straight, to crush down the uneven places in life.

He decided that there should be a way to add culture to the lives of his subjects. His method was the public arena. There, humans and beasts performed before audiences. But his fancies asserted themselves here. The arena that he built was not for the honor and glory of gladiators. It was not for beasts to fight each other to the finish. It was not even for throwing religious heretics to the lions. It was, he believed, for the purpose of widening and developing the mental energies of his people. It was a vast amphitheater with encircling galleries, mysterious vaults, and unseen passages. It was to be a means for poetic justice. It was to be a place where crime was punished or virtue rewarded—all by chance.

When the king was interested in people and their crimes, he would dictate that their fate should be decided in the arena. This king knew no traditions from other kingdoms. His only allegiance was to himself and his own fancies. This fancy, the chance-fate decision in the arena, came about because of his romantic, yet barbaric, idealism.

When all the people had gathered in the galleries and the king was seated on his throne high up on one side of the arena, he would give a signal. A door beneath him would open, and the accused person would step out into the amphitheater. Directly opposite the accused there were two doors, exactly alike and side by side. The person on trial had to walk over to these doors and open one of them. He could open whichever door he wanted; he was subject to no pressure from the king or his court. The only influence was that of fate or luck.

If the accused opened one door, a hungry tiger came out. It was the fiercest and most cruel that could be found, and it immediately jumped on him and tore him to pieces as a punishment for his guilt. When the fate of the criminal was thus decided, sad iron bells were rung, and great wails went up from the hired mourners who were posted outside the arena. The audience went home with bowed heads and doleful hearts, sad that one so young and fair (or so old and respected) should have merited such a fate.

If he opened the other door, a lady came out. The king always chose the ladies himself. He made sure that each was of the same age and station as the accused and that she was beautiful. The rule was that the accused was to marry her immediately. It didn't matter if he were already married and had a family. The lady was a sign of his innocence, so if the accused already loved another, that other was to be forgotten. It was the king's way. He allowed nothing to interfere with his design. Indeed, immediately after the lady appeared, another door beneath the king opened and out came a priest, musicians, singers, and a troupe of dancers. In a procession, they all cheerfully marched and sang for the couple standing in the middle of the arena. The bells rang, the audience shouted its approval, and the innocent man, preceded by children strewing flowers in the couple's path, led his new bride to his home.

This was the king's semibarbaric method of administering justice, and its fairness is obvious. The criminal could not know which door the lady was behind. He opened whichever door he wanted to without knowing whether in the next instant he was to be eaten or married. On some occasions the tiger came out of one door, and on other occasions it came out of the other. In this system, there was instant punishment for guilt and instant reward for innocence—whether the accused wanted the reward or not. There was no escape from the judgment of the king's arena.

The institution was a popular one. When the people gathered together on one of the trial days, they never knew whether they were to witness a bloody slaughter or a festive wedding. This element of uncertainty usually made the occasion more interesting than it would have been otherwise. The people were entertained, and no one doubted that justice was being served. All believed that the accused had his fate in his own hands.

Comprehension

1. What was the king like?
2. How was he different from his neighbors?
3. Why did he build the arena? What did it look like?
4. How did the system begin on trial days?
5. What did the accused have to do?
6. What happened if he chose the door with a tiger behind it?
7. What happened if he chose the other door?
8. What made these trial days popular?
9. Was this system fair? Why?
10. Why do you think the people liked this system of justice?

PART TWO

The semibarbaric king had a daughter whom he loved deeply. She was as passionate, fanciful, and strong as her father and was devoted to him. As is the case in many fairy tales, this daughter, the apple of her father's eye, was in love with a young man who was below her in station. He was a commoner. He was also brave, handsome, and daring, and he loved the royal daughter with all his being. The princess had enough barbarism in her that their love affair was dramatic . . . too dramatic. It was a secret for months, but then the king found out about it.

The king didn't hesitate for a minute. He sent the young man to prison and set a date for his trial in the arena. When the date arrived, everyone in the kingdom wanted to attend. They all knew of the king's interest in the case, and there was excitement in the air.

The king's men searched for the fiercest tiger in the realm. They also searched for the fairest maiden in the land so that he could have a fitting bride in case he were found innocent. Of course, everyone knew that he had committed the "crime" of loving the princess, but the king did not allow the facts of the case to alter his decision. The trial would go on as planned. The youth would be gone no matter what happened; he would either be dead or married. The king could enjoy the proceedings for the sport of it.

The day arrived. The people were standing in every corner of the arena. All was ready when the moment came. A signal was given and the door opened, allowing the princess' lover to enter. The crowd gasped. He was handsome. Half the audience did not know that one so attractive had lived among them; no wonder the princess loved him! How terrible for him to be there!

The princess had thought about this trial day and night for a long time. She knew she couldn't bear to miss the spectacle, but there was another reason for her being there. She had such power, influence, and force of character (as well as plenty of gold) that she did what no one had ever done before; she found out the secret of the doors for that day. She knew in which room stood the hungry tiger and in which waited the lady. She knew, too, that the doors were so thick that there was no way anyone could ever hear some hint from behind them. If she were going to warn her lover, she would have to do it by signal.

She also knew something which made the whole process more complicated. She knew that the lady was one of the most beautiful maidens in the whole country, and the thought of her young man living with this woman enraged her. She hated the lady and hated what might happen.

When the accused bowed to the royal box, as was the custom, he looked only at the princess, and immediately he knew. He had expected her to find out the secret of the doors, and now he knew that she had the answer. It was only left for her to tell him.

His quick glance at her asked, "Which?" It was as plain as if he had shouted it. There was no time to lose; the quick question had to be answered just as quickly so that the king would not suspect.

Her right hand was resting on a pillow in front of her. She raised it slightly and made a small, fast movement to the right. No one but her lover saw her. Every eye in the arena was fixed on him.

He turned, and with a firm and rapid step he walked across the empty space. Every heart stopped beating, every breath was held, every eye was upon him. Without hesitation, he went to the door on the right and opened it.

Did the tiger come out of that door, or did the lady?

The more we think about this question, the harder it is to answer. It involves a study of the human heart which leads to mazes of passion, love, hate, and excitement. Do not answer this for yourself, but put yourself in the place of the princess.

She was hot-blooded and semibarbaric, and her soul burned with the twin desires of longing and jealousy. She knew that she had already lost him. But to whom?

How often she had lain awake at night imagining the horror of her lover being killed by a tiger! Even in her dreams, she had covered her face with her hands to hide from the cruelty.

But how much more often had she seen him at the other door! In her mind she had screamed and torn her hair when she saw his happy face at opening the door to the lady. Her soul burned in agony as she saw him rush to that woman and then be wedded in the next moment, when all about her were joyous. She lived through the misery of the procession, the happy couple, the singing and dancing, the shouts of the crowd, the laughter of the wandering children. Her tears, of course, were lost in all the joy.

Would it be better for him to die at once? Then he could go to the place after death and wait for her.

And yet, that awful tiger, those shrieks, that blood!

Her decision had been made in the instant that she moved her hand. She had known that he would ask, but she had put off her decision until the last moment. She finally decided, and without hesitation, she indicated the right-hand door.

This is not a question to be taken lightly. Her decision was serious for her, so I do not presume to answer for her. I leave it to all of you. Which came out of the opened door—the lady, or the tiger?

Comprehension and Discussion

1. What was the king's daughter like? How was she similar to her father?
2. Why did the king send his daughter's lover to prison?
3. Why did he think that he would be rid of the young man no matter what happened?
4. Why was the audience surprised when the young man entered the arena?
5. What had the princess discovered about the doors?
6. Describe the silent communication between the young man and the princess.
7. What did the princess imagine when she saw her lover open the tiger door? The lady door?
8. What do you think of this system of justice? Is fate the best way to decide guilt or innocence?
9. What deeper message do you think the author had which he was trying to communicate to us?
10. What came out of the opened door? If you were the princess, which choice would you have made?

Exercises

A. Use each of the following terms in a sentence:
   moral, psychological, gruff, at least, gladiator, religious, heretic, by chance, whichever, to be posted, slaughter, to be in one's own hands, the apple of one's eye, spectacle, to put oneself in the place of, hot-blooded, semibarbaric, without hesitation, right-hand.

B. Fill in the blanks with the appropriate form of the adjective.

Example: It was the _____ (long), _____
_____ (difficult) question I ever had to answer.
(It was the longest, most difficult question I ever
had to answer.)

1. They searched for the _____ (fierce)
   tiger in the realm.
2. She was the _____ (beautiful) maiden
   in the kingdom.
3. The king was _____ (tall) than his
   daughter.
4. The princess was _____ (barbaric) as
   her father.
5. The people gasped because they thought he was the
   _____ (handsome) young man they had
   ever seen.
6. It was the _____ (cruel) tiger they could
   find.
7. The princess thought that the lady was _____
   _____ (beautiful) than she was.
8. They couldn't find any system of justice which was
   _____ (fair) than this one.
9. I don't think that this crowd is _____
   (large) as the crowd we had last week.
10. Which possibility made the princess _____
    (angry), the lady, or the tiger?

C. Circle the word on the right that has a SIMILAR meaning
   to the word on the left.

   Example: in back of   across/(behind)/after/ with

   1. hitch   snag/food/weather/walk
   2. troupe   group/pair/loop/several
   3. passionate   easygoing/aware/intense/available.
   4. alter   use/eat/marry/change
   5. hint   clue/speech/delivery/desire
   6. often   seldom/frequent/never/always
   7. shriek   laugh/talk/cry/indicate
   8. crude   open/new/unsophisticated/old
   9. gruff   pleasant/happy/enthusiastic/rough
   10. arena   stage/stadium/kingdom/vault

D. Change these sentences first to the future with *will*, then to
   the future with *going to.*

86

Example: He goes on trial tomorrow.
              (He will go on trial tomorrow.)
              (He is going to go on trial tomorrow.)

1. She signals with her right hand.
2. She discovered the secret of the doors.
3. They cheer when there is a wedding.
4. We stand when the king enters the arena.
5. I was present at the trial.
6. You decide which came out of the door.
7. He walked immediately to the door on the right.
8. He knew his fate was behind one of the doors.
9. The stories have deep moral implications.
10. She screamed and tore her hair.

Unit 11: Adolescence

Hetty Hemingway

Hetty Hemingway wrote many short stories for her friends and family, but this was the only one for the general public.

PART ONE

Sara and Polly always seemed to dawdle a few feet behind their governess. They constantly exchanged meaningful glances, and they were always smiling at each other and squeezing hands.

Mrs. White walked briskly in front of them, but she constantly twisted her head around like a mother goose. Her voice sounded harsh and concerned. "What are you girls babbling about there? I declare, we will never see Naples at this rate! Here we are at the National Museum, and instead of looking at things, you're always whispering and laughing. We might just as well be back in the convent. I will never take two such heedless young things traveling again!"

The governess spoke with a vehemence that she tried to make sound convincing. It was difficult. In the course of her whole drab, prosaic life she had never had so much pleasure as now. It was such a treat to leave her crabbed and invalided old mother, to whom she was devoted, and take these two rich girls from the convent traveling in Italy. Yet she repeated very often, "I declare, I will never take young girls traveling again! Such responsibility! I'm exhausted. It's terrible, terrible."

She announced that they were going to see the Pompeian relics. "Oh, yes, we must see them; they are very important for your education. Oh! Polly, what are you looking at now?"

Polly was standing before a figure of the Hermes of Praxiteles. She had let go of Sara's hand.

"Come, don't look at that," said the governess, hastily consulting her guidebook. "It's only a plaster cast; it's not the real thing. Now, that Minerva over there, it was—" She began to read.

But Polly wasn't interested in the Minerva. She gave it a perfunctory glance, and her soft eyes reverted and lingered with unfathomable admiration on the white, graceful messenger god. He regarded her, as he regarded everything in the room, with his smile, mysterious and aloof, of disdainful tenderness.

"What are those impudent young men over there laughing at?" cried Mrs. White. "Don't turn around, Sara. One doesn't smile at strange men in Italy."

Sara turned around, of course, and stared with interest at the three young men.

"I think they probably like our looks," said Sara, who always spoke the truth. She was a beautiful seventeen-year-old, with the touching and sheltered purity of a little child.

Certainly the men were looking at Polly, just as she was looking at the Hermes, smiling to herself and humming. The sunlight, spilling through a stained-glass window, spattered his dazzling body with multicolored light.

The governess cleared her throat, startling Polly in her reverie. The three ladies proceeded to the Pompeian room.

Later, they lunched on the open terrace of a hotel overlooking the bay, with Vesuvius puffing in the distance.

"Oh, how splendid! How spectacular!" Mrs. White seemed to be muttering or exclaiming about everything they saw. It exasperated her that Sara and Polly took as much pleasure in their meal as they did in the view. The governess somehow believed that she must always be expressing aloud her appreciation of beautiful things. She spoke as if to some unseen creator who needed to hear her. She was like a tiresome dinner guest who is constantly thanking and complimenting her host. Sara and Polly, on the other hand, accepted beauty and drank it in without self-consciousness. Children somehow share the marvelous egotism of gods in this respect. Whatever was there was the natural background and scenery for themselves, so they scarcely thought of it.

After lunch they drove to a monastery described in the guidebook under "Interesting Sights." It was perched on the side of a dusty hill, and its white spires gleamed among the vineyards with a full, azure-blue Neapolitan sky above. An old monk, dressed in a brown, hooded cloak with a rope around its waist, showed them about the place. As he moved, his great ring of keys bounced and jingled.

Inside the gray walls was a mellow hush, an immaculate stillness. The sunlight inundated the court, falling hot on the flagstones between the white pillars of the cloisters, where other brown-clad brothers were walking sadly, their eyes fixed on the ground. Sara and Polly thought that they had never beheld such abundant sunshine or such deep shadows or known such stillness. Their hearts were full of awe and reverence because of the sun and the silence and the brown brothers walking sadly with their eyes on the ground. Even Mrs. White was impressed, and she read from her guidebook in a hushed, monotonous tone, as if it were the breviary.

"We must see the crypt. It says the mosaics are of special interest. It says the underground passages are more interesting, on a smaller scale, than the Catacombs at Rome," she whispered to the girls.

The cold breath of the crypt fanned their faces as they descended the sunken stone steps. Underneath the chapel the air felt stale and fuzzy. They were in the crypt of the church. Polly looked at Sara, at her calm, deep, Madonna-like face. All around them, piled against the ornate walls, were bones and skeletons. They were tossed about in no particular method or order. Empty heads stared at them from dark corners, and there was a dank odor that made their flesh creep.

"This is how we shall all be eventually," said the old monk in a reverent tone. Sara closed her eyes, smiling, and clasped her hands tightly together. Even Mrs. White was affected. Polly looked about her at the gleaming, hollow heads and imagined that they were leering at her. She took a deep breath of the stale, lifeless air. Quite suddenly an armless, legless skeleton reminded her of the statue she had seen that morning. A great wave of ecstatic buoyancy leaped within her.

"I'm young, young, young," she cried to herself, bracing her tingling feet against the stone floor as if she could draw life like a plant from the earth, rich with the ashes of countless dead. She looked at the sagging face of the governess in the green light and the lined, parchment countenance of the old monk, and she continued to thrill and to tingle and to cry to herself, "I'm young, young, young; I shall never die—never, never, never!" She smiled impudently and coyly into the graves dotted with white heads. She caught the old monk's glowing eye upon her, and he seemed to divine her mood, for all at once he threw back his head, and his old eyes glowed and lighted.

"Long live the young! Life to the young!" he cried, raising the torch high and saluting Polly playfully with it. "Our Savior, too, was young and knew the joy of life," he added, crossing himself and smiling tenderly and oddly.

"These brothers!" said the governess when they were back in their carriage, rattling along the dusty road. "I don't trust them. They're full of tricks. I don't even trust the gray hairs, children," she added with a cunning, satisfied expression. She smiled curiously and decided on the spot that they would not spend the evening at the hotel going to bed early. She mulled it over in her mind, looking mysterious all through dinner. At dessert she said, "You girls go up and put on your best dresses. We're going to the opera."

Comprehension

1. What is the relationship among the three main characters?
2. Where are they? Why are they there?
3. Why did Polly stand before the statue of Hermes and stare?
4. Why were the young men staring at Polly?
5. How did the two young girls react to nature and beauty?
6. Why did they go to the monastery?
7. Describe the monastery.

8. Why did they go to the crypt? What was it like?
9. What happened to Polly as she was standing in the crypt looking at a skeleton?
10. How did the monk respond to Polly's mood?

PART TWO

Sara wore a white dress and put a blue ribbon in her hair. Polly put on a white dress because Sara had done so, and she put a blue ribbon in her hair,too. She was distressed because the shade of blue was slightly paler than Sara's. All the way in the carriage she held Sara's cool, smooth hand. It was necessary for the perfection of her happiness that she should be near or touching Sara all the time. It relieved a happiness which was almost too great for her to bear alone. She often felt happy and elated for no reason she could explain. During the drive, her fifteen-year-old heart gave her sensations that, in a grown-up person, would have been cause enough to send for a doctor.

Mrs. White wore a stiff, black silk dress. Money from her savings had been taken to buy it. A great deal of anxious thought had gone into it. To the girls, it looked exactly as any black silk dress would look on a stout, elderly woman; but to Mrs. White, who had never had anything pretty to wear, it was deliciously important. She was as concerned about it as if she were still young and good-looking.

Sara and Polly had never been in a theater as large as the one in Naples. They were thrilled by the vastness and all the ornate trimmings. They adored the pale blue ceiling which was painted in imitation of the sky, with white clouds and angels floating across it. Sara loved the idea of painting one's ceiling to look like the sky and was smiling at the angels when she heard a Frenchwoman, who looked very intellectual, say, "What taste! Look at that ridiculous ceiling!"

Both Sara and Polly wondered how anyone could be so blind to beauty.

The opera was in Italian, and Polly could not understand one word that the actors were saying, but she was vaguely and exquisitely entertained just the same. She felt instinctively that the story was improper, but the fact did not interest her.

The music made all the trivialities on the stage seem romantic. Every time the hero, who was a little fop in a red fez with something ludicrous in his motions, approached the heroine, the

92

orchestra played the "Waltz Dream." The melody began in a low key, swelling higher and higher, repeating and intensifying its poignant refrain, till it became so pleading and insistent that the audience began to sway with it. Some persons nodded their heads or tapped their feet; others lay back in their chairs and smiled dreamily with closed eyes.

In a box, elevated over the stage at one side, Polly recognized an Italian officer she had seen at the museum. He was resplendent in a pale-blue uniform; the metal trappings on his coat and sword reflected the light of the stage and twinkled like multicolored jewels in the semidarkness of the orchestra. His head was fair and large and shaped like that of the Hermes of Praxiteles. His lips wore the same expression of aloof and slightly mocking tenderness. When the "Waltz Dream" was played, he stood up and, with his arm about a comrade, swayed his slim body with the rhythm of the music. There was an elemental and spontaneous grace in the unselfconscious motions which told anyone whose eye happened to follow the sinuous figure that he was intoxicated with the music, that he felt its caressing and insistent melody running through him.

Polly, from her seat in the dark orchestra, kept turning her eyes in the direction of the swaying figure in the box. She felt the music running through her, too. She squeezed Sara's hand, but it did not satisfy or console her entirely. The wistfulness of her mood, induced by the music, seemed to her to become so vast as to be almost unendurable. It was as if the persistent burden of the song were reminding her of something forgotten, something once known and amazing, an intimate mystery, poignant, beautiful, and unfinished.

The music subsided softly. The curtain dropped while the audience applauded. The opera was over. There was a sudden stampede for cloaks and hats. Sara and Polly were jostled by the crowd. Mrs. White spoke loudly and angrily, as she always did when she was frightened. The girls laughed.

Suddenly Polly cried out as a strange hand from the crowd passed swiftly yet caressingly over her bare neck and down between her shoulder blades. She felt fingers gently clasp her small neck and shake her playfully. She also heard a laughing voice whispering, "Cattiva, cattiva, Bimba mia!"

Polly shrank backwards into Sara and turned quickly to see who was at the end of that hand and voice. "Look at that man!

See what he did to me!" She cried out indignantly. "He put his hand right down my back!"

"It was the same officer who was standing in the box over the stage. I saw him!" exclaimed Sara.

Polly was hot all over, and tears rose in her eyes.

"It's your own fault," Mrs. White said as she signaled for a carriage. "Why did you stare at him during the entire performance? I saw you, you know. What do you expect? You can't do things like that in Italy."

Finally they found a cab. Mrs. White was exhausted by this time and she promptly fell asleep in a corner of the seat, her head nodding on her breast. Polly held Sara's hand again and watched her Madonna-like face, pure in the flickering light of the passing street lamps.

"I'm so tired," murmured Sara. "You know, Polly, I think it would be lovely to live in a monastery—I mean a convent—like the one we saw this afternoon, don't you? I would love to die young and beautiful, wouldn't you?"

Polly thought about it, but didn't answer. She wondered how anyone could possibly be tired. She thought about the monastery, and she remembered again the wave of ecstatic life that had welled up within her as she looked at the poor armless skeleton. No, she did not wish to die young; her little body and soul were exquisitely troubled by the presence of an energy which was rampant within her. It was more significant and alive than she was herself.

Her eyes were dreamy, but not with sleep. Later, as they were getting ready for bed, she sat in one position for at least ten minutes, caressingly passing her fingers through her unbound hair.

She lay beside Sara in the dark for a long time, not moving. Softly she crept out of bed, and lighting the pink light by the dressing table, she looked over her shoulder and surveyed her plump neck above the thin shoulder blades. Reverently and cautiously she passed her hand over them.

She turned out the lights and, going to the open window, laid her head upon the sill. Oh, the Bay of Naples, rippling in the moonlight, and Vesuvius, serene and terrible, clothed in the starlit mist and darkness! The sweet, sweet fragrance of the spring, rising from the orange blossoms—all this! But Polly did not see the Bay of Naples or even mighty Vesuvius, mounting alive out of the night. She was only vaguely aware of the teeming scent from the pale, closed buds below. She was thinking of a smile of disdainful tenderness, of a caress arrogant and fleeting. Her dumb little being was stirred and jarred by a stupendous wonder, and there was spring in the fifteen-year-old heart that night.

Comprehension and Discussion

1. What did Polly and Sara wear to the opera?
2. What was significant about Mrs. White's dress?
3. What was interesting about the theater?
4. Describe the music of the opera and its effect on the audience.
5. What was the officer whom Polly watched doing during the play?
6. What happened as the girls left the theater?
7. What was Mrs. White's reaction to the incident?
8. What were Polly's thoughts as she lay in bed that night?
9. Do you think most fifteen-year-olds feel emotions similar to those of Polly?
10. What stage of life was Polly passing through? What is/was this like for you?

Exercises

A. Use each of the following terms in a sentence:
   to dawdle, to squeeze, briskly, to babble, prosaic, relic, unfathomable, to spatter, dazzling, egotism, scarcely, to be perched on, to jingle, fuzzy, dank, hollow, to leer, skeleton, ecstatic, on the spot, trimming, stout, ornate, spontaneous, indignant.

B. Supply the appropriate tag ending for each of these statements.

   Example: You're going to the opera.
             (You're going to the opera, aren't you?)

   1. I don't have to go there.
   2. They're full of tricks.
   3. He was always smiling at her.
   4. She wasn't wearing a white dress tonight.
   5. Mrs. White isn't an Italian.
   6. You can't understand that opera.
   7. We'll take the carriage to go to the theater.
   8. The play won't be over until eleven o'clock.

9. Sara would love to live in a convent.
10. Sara wouldn't want to live there alone.

C. Match the word in the left column with the word most SIMILAR to it in the right column.

Example: e 1. adore   e. love

   ___ 1. adore   a. dreamy
   ___ 2. dank   b. quickly
   ___ 3. wistful   c. drunk
   ___ 4. ecstatic   d. old
   ___ 5. briskly   e. love
   ___ 6. significant   f. meaningful
   ___ 7. creator   g. damp
   ___ 8. intoxicated   h. joyous
   ___ 9. elderly   i. silly
   ___ 10. ridiculous   j. maker

D. Change the following sentences first to the present perfect tense and then to the present perfect continuous tense.

Example: She was thinking about it.
           (She has thought about it.)
           (She has been thinking about it.)

1. She stood before that statue.
2. They are visiting Italy.
3. She sat beside Sara in the carriage.
4. What are you doing?
5. The officer spoke to her.
6. They saw churches and museums.
7. The sunlight fell on the flagstones of the cloisters.
8. They exchanged meaningful glances.
9. Mrs. White spoke to them harshly.
10. They were listening to the music.

Unit 12: The Gifts of Feodor Himkoff

A. Quiller-Couch

Sir Arthur Quiller-Couch (1863–1944) was a popular romantic writer at the turn of the century. He taught at Cambridge University and was well known for his translations of fairy tales.

PART ONE

It has been six years since I first traveled to the coast from my home in Gorrans Point. Since then I have visited it in all kinds of foul weather. Perhaps in time, I'll be able to make the journey blindfolded, the way the coastguardsmen do. But to this day, my most memorable visit was that time I went there in December. It was my first visit, and it was truly memorable. It was also a rude introduction to the area. The wind blew in my face, covering me with cold rain. A heavy fog hung low over the channel, hiding everything in its path like a leaden mist. Occasionally the fog parted enough to show the white zigzag of ocean breakers and a patch of land. I also saw a cluster of rocks below with the sea crawling in between, disrupting the weeds. It was a harsh scene.

The image, which is with me even today, is mostly one of wet bushes, puffs of spray from the ocean rising above the cliffs to cover me, and a total grayness all about me.

Beyond the Nare Head, where the path dipped steeply, I saw a bright square which seemed to be shaking itself loose from the mist. I approached to investigate and found that it was a cottage wedged between the footpath and the sea. It would be hard to imagine a more desolate place to put a house. It looked forbidding, but the fire's glow from within attracted me. It almost invited me through its cheery warmth. I decided to risk stopping and asking for a glass of milk. I also longed to meet some of the local people.

An old woman answered my knock. She was tall and slightly stooped, and her complexion was a sickly-looking yellow. She wore a clean white cap which almost—but not quite—hid her gray locks. She also wore a gray housedress which hung below her knees and thick woolen stockings. But she wore no shoes.

"A glass of milk? Why not a cup of hot tea?"

"I don't want to put you to any trouble," I said, although I wanted to feel the warmth of a hot liquid in my stomach.

"No one ever puts us to any trouble, young man. We're only too glad to be able to help a cold soul in need. Step inside by the fire. There's only my old husband and me here. You won't be any trouble for us. Just sit anywhere. The old man's deaf.

"Isaac," she fairly shouted, "here's a stranger who's come to visit us." The man she called Isaac was huddled and nodding in a chair before the fire. He looked up at me but didn't seem too curious, then he closed his eyes and slept again. He was obviously nearing the end of his days. He had no hearing facility. He seemed to be waiting to die.

My boots were so muddy that they made great soiling marks on the woman's newly scrubbed floor. In spite of this, she dusted the chair where I was to sit as though I were royalty. She put a pot of water on the stove to heat and took a lovely small cup from the shelf above the hearth. Then she took a key from a hook near the cupboard, climbed on a chair, and reached to the top of the highest closet in the room. I offered to help her get whatever she was looking for, but she declined my offer, saying she could manage for herself. Finally, she brought down a small green canister.

I wish I could describe the tea that came from this canister. Its fragrance filled the air immediately as the boiling water was poured over it. Even the old man in his sleep stirred as the rich aroma filled his nose. The woman poured a cup, and I sipped it.

Smuggled, I thought to myself, enjoying it more and more with each sip. No one could get tea like this back in London for less than fifty shillings a pound, and these people were not rich . . .

"Do you like it?" she asked. Before I could answer, she started bringing down all sorts of delicacies from the cupboard. The contents of that cupboard! Caviar came from it as well as a small ambrosial cheese. She also brought out dried figs and guava jelly, olives, cherries in brandy, wonderful filberts covered with sugar, biscuits, and a lot of different Russian sweets. I leaned back with wide eyes.

"Feodor sends us these," said the old woman, bringing a dish of Cornish cream and some homemade bread.

"Who's Feodor?"

"Feodor Himkoff." She paused a moment and then added, "He's a sailor on a Russian vessel."

"A friend?"

The question was ignored. "Is there anything in particular you'd like to have to eat?" she asked. "We've got some fine and interesting foods."

"Do you like these things?" I looked from her to the caviar and wondered about the tastes of these simple people.

"I don't know. I never tried any of them. The only reason we keep them around is for folks like yourself who might come to visit unexpectedly."

"But these are dainty delicacies. They belong on rich people's tables." I hoped I wasn't offending her.

"I wouldn't know. I've never tasted them. I'm afraid they'd stick in my throat."

I wanted to ask dozens of questions, but I decided that it would be impolite, so I held my silence. After a short while, when we both sat in silence, I looked up and noticed her eyes fixed on me. I put down my knife.

"I can't help it," I said. "I have to know about Feodor Himkoff."

Comprehension

1. When did the narrator first visit the coast?
2. Describe the weather on his first visit.
3. Why did he want to go into the cottage?
4. Describe the old woman who answered the door.
5. Who was Isaac? What was he doing when the narrator entered the house?
6. Why did the old woman climb up on a chair?
7. What was special about the tea in the green canister?
8. What did the woman put on the table in addition to the cup of tea?
9. What was unusual about the food?
10. Why did the narrator want to know about Feodor Himkoff?

PART TWO

"There's no secret," she began. "Well, there was once, but God has forgiven us by now, I'm sure. That old man has done all the repenting he's ever going to do."

She waited a few long seconds and then went on.

"We had a son. He was a fine young man. He stood tall. He joined the army and was killed by Russians—Rooshans, we used to call them. Look at the frail old man. When this news came, he wasn't so frail and weak. He lifted his fists to the sun and said, 'God help me . . . God help him, if I ever come across a Rooshan! I hope I find one! I hope God sends me one—just one!' The boy was our only child.

"Well, sir, sixteen years went by, and the two of us were sitting here by the fire on a night just like tonight. The storm was worse that night, though. There was so much noise that we had to shout just to hear each other. About ten o'clock we heard a banging on the door, so Isaac got up and opened it, asking, 'Who is it?'

"There was a big young man at the door, dripping wet, with smears of blood on his face and a fearful look in his eyes. His voice sounded foreign, and it was very low and hard to hear, but when he saw our fire, his eyes lit up and he smiled so that we could see teeth like pearls.

" 'Ah, sir,' he cried, 'will you help? Our ship is ashore below here. There are fifteen of us. Please send for help! Please help us!'

"Isaac stepped back and spoke softly. 'What country?'

" 'The ship is Russian. We are all Russian; sixteen poor brothers from Archangel,' said the young man as soon as he understood the question.

"Isaac turned his back on the man and walked over to the fire. The sailor stretched out his hands, and I saw that his middle finger was gone. 'You will help us, won't you? There are so many of us who need help. Many have wives. The storm . . .'

"But Isaac didn't hear. He was looking upward saying, 'Thank you, Lord,' and he picked up a log from the fire. 'Take them this message,' he said as he raced toward the sailor with a burning stick. The young man was so weak he couldn't fight back. Isaac hit him with the log and chased him out the door. Then he bolted it.

"After that we sat quietly all through the night, never undressing and getting into bed. At daybreak Isaac walked down to the shore. There was nothing to see but two bodies, so he buried them both and waited for more. That evening another came in from the sea, and the next day two more, and so on for seven more days. He picked up ten bodies in all and buried them in that meadow down there. On the fourth day he found a body with a missing finger. It was the boy he had driven from our home. Isaac buried him, too. And that was all, except for two more bodies which the coast guard found later that month.

"For five years neither Isaac nor I spoke of the incident, not even to each other. And then one day at noon a sailor came to our door. He looked foreign and had a great beard.

" 'I be come to see Mr. Isaac Lenine,' he said in his bad English.

"So I called for Isaac, and the stranger gripped him by the hands and kissed them, saying, 'Little Father, take me to their graves. My name is Feodor Himkoff, and my brother Dimitri was among the crew of the *Viatka*. You would know his body if you buried it, for the second finger was gone from his right hand. I, myself, caused the accident in which he lost that finger; we were playing with an ax when we were children. I heard how the men from the ship died in a storm, how they perished far from help of any kind. I heard how you buried them in your own field. I have prayed to all the saints for you.'

"So Isaac led him to the field and showed him his brother's grave, which Isaac had marked along with all the rest. God help my poor man, he was too much a coward to speak. So the Russian stayed with us until evening, and he kissed us both on

both cheeks and went away blessing us. Oh, God forgive us!
God forgive us!

"Ever since then, he's been sending us precious packages
through the post office. Wonderful things such as these." She
stopped her story and went to Isaac to make sure that he was
comfortable in his chair.

"It's all we can do to get rid of them by giving them to
travelers like yourself."

Comprehension and Discussion

1. What happened to the old woman's son?
2. Why did the old man wish that God would send him a
   Russian?
3. Why did the young Russian sailor appear at their door?
4. What did Isaac do when he found out that the sailor was
   Russian?
5. When did Isaac go down to the shore? What did he do
   when he got there?
6. Who was the person who went to their home five years
   later? What did he want?
7. Why did the brother start to send the Lenines packages of
   delicious food?
8. What did the author of this story want to tell us?
9. How do you feel about the anger and desire for revenge
   which Isaac felt?
10. What are some delicate, expensive foods which you have
    tried? Have you tasted any of those mentioned in the story?

Exercises

A. Use each of the following terms in a sentence:
foul weather, blindfolded, memorable, zigzag, ocean
breaker, desolate, complexion, a soul in need, deaf, royalty,
hearth, canister, aroma, smuggled, delicacy, homemade, to
repent, frail, log, meadow, incident, ax, too much a coward,
to get rid of something.

B. Fill in the blanks in the following sentences with one of the
terms from the list.

Example: I don't recognize the ____taste (noun)____ of this
food.

102

still (adjective)	smile (noun)	see
still (adverb)	smile (verb)	sea
war	taste (noun)	
wore	taste (verb)	

1. I don't like the _____ of caviar.
2. The sailors didn't _____ while they were fighting the storm. They looked serious.
3. Our son went away to fight in the _____.
4. He came to the door with a broad _____ on his face.
5. The poor man _____ a dirty old coat which was ripped.
6. I can _____ that you and your companions are in need of help.
7. These foods _____ like delicacies.
8. The _____ can be treacherous when the fog is this thick.
9. We sat very _____ for a long time.
10. At dawn we were _____ sitting by the fire with our clothes on.

C. Match the term in the left column with its OPPOSITE in the right column.

Example: c **1.** wonderful   **c.** terrible

___	**1.** wonderful	**a.** clothed
___	**2.** first	**b.** visible
___	**3.** frail	**c.** terrible
___	**4.** fresh (fruit)	**d.** sunny
___	**5.** naked	**e.** strong
___	**6.** loose	**f.** tight
___	**7.** hidden	**g.** last
___	**8.** foggy	**h.** silence
___	**9.** noise	**i.** dawn
___	**10.** dusk	**j.** dried

D. Change the verbs in the following sentences to the past continuous tense. Add additional phrases.

Example: They sat by the fire.
(They were sitting by the fire when someone knocked at the door.)

1. The man walked along the footpath.

103

2. He traveled to the coast from his home in Gorrans Point.
3. The wind blew in his face.
4. She didn't wear any shoes.
5. Isaac slept in a chair in front of the fire.
6. She poured the boiling water over the tea.
7. I wondered about the tastes of these simple people.
8. Her son fought in the army.
9. The two of us drank tea.
10. I listened to her story.